WWBD?
what would betty do?

*how to succeed at
the expense of others
in this world and the next*

Paul A. Bradley

A Fireside Book
Published by Simon & Schuster
New York   London   Toronto   Sydney   Singapore

FIRESIDE
Rockefeller Center
1230 Avenue of the Americas
New York, NY 10020

True Christian™ is a registered trademark of Mrs. Betty Bowers. Betty Bowers® and Betty Bowers, America's Best Christian® are registered trademarks of Paul A. Bradley.

FIRESIDE and colophon are registered trademarks of Simon & Schuster Inc.

For information about special discounts for bulk purchases, please contact Simon & Schuster Special Sales at 1-800-456-6798 or business@simonandschuster.com

Designed by Bonni Leon

Manufactured in the United States of America

10 9 8 7 6 5 4 3 2 1

Library of Congress Cataloging-in-Publication Data
Bradley, Paul A.
    What would Betty do? : how to succeed at the expense of others in this world and the next / Paul A. Bradley.
        p.   cm.
    1. Christian life—Miscellanea. I. Title: WWBD?. II. Title.
    BV4501.3 .B74   2002
    277.3'083'0207—dc21   2004055598

ISBN 7432-1601-6

Enthusiastic, yet decorous, hosannas to Jody, Trish, Kris, Chris, Brian, Erik, Theresa, Jim and Abbe, but mostly to John and Anastatia.

—America's Best Christian

Contents

Meet the Author   15
Introduction   17

W W B H *what would betty have?*

the appearance of absolute marital submission—and then her own way!

Bringing Integrity To Christian Homemakers   19
From the Diary of America's Best Christian:
   Protecting Yourself from Celestial Voyeurs   20
B.I.T.C.H. Submission Muzzles Have Arrived Just in Time for
   This Sunday's Services!   21
Epistle of Profound and Compassionate Christian Advice:
   Getting Restraining Orders Against Intrusive Guardian Angels   22
Pews News: Mrs. Betty Bowers Flies a Planeload of B.I.T.C.H.s to Italy   25
Epistle of Profound and Compassionate Christian Advice:
   Salvation Through Skin Care   26

W W B R *what would betty read?*

her autographed bible—and then her friends for their ill-conceived look!

Epistle of Profound and Compassionate Christian Advice:
   Using the Old Testament to Your Advantage   29
Betty's Handy True Christian™ Guide to Biblical Interpretation   31
Epistle of Profound and Compassionate Christian Advice:
   Are You Keeping Track of How Many Times You Are Born Again?   32
Christian BS: Bible Study. The Gospel According to Mrs. Betty Bowers   34

WWBD *what won't betty do?*

in her walk-in closet, anything twice—in her marital bed, anything once

Saving Love Until The Sacrament   35

Is the Bible Too Smutty for a Christian Home?   35

God Created Adam and His Wife, Eve—Not Adam and
    His Domestic Partner, Steve   38

Biblically Correct Sexual Survival Tips   39

An Apple Was Not the Only Forbidden Thing the Trollop Eve Put in Her Mouth:
    The Sexual Escapades of This Planet's First Family   41

Epistle of Profound and Compassionate Christian Advice:
    Whom Did Mary Have Sex With?   42

Betty's Ex Cathedra Encyclical on Same-Sex Marriage   43

When It Comes to Sex, a Baptist Lady Never Does Anything That . . .   44

WWBH *who would betty help?*

not the so-called homeless—but herself to another beluga toast point!

CHARITY: Sometimes Jesus Calls Upon Us to Acknowledge
    Even the Truly Dreadful   45

From the Diary of America's Best Christian: Finding Starvation's Silver Lining   46

Epistle of Profound and Compassionate Christian Advice: The Poor Will
    Always Be with Us, So We Needn't Break a Heel Rushing to Help Them   48

Betty Bowers' Christian Crack Whore Ministry   50

WWBT *what would betty throw?*

a soirée and then a few stones!

Imaginative Ways the Lord Has Killed or Otherwise Inconvenienced People   52

Having the Honor of Casting the First Stone   55

State Executions: America's Timid Replication of Old Testament Wrath   56

Who Would Betty Stone?: A Handy Checklist So No Sinner Feels Left Out   57

WWBS *what would betty save?*

her monthly quota of souls—and then herself the embarrassment of ascending to heaven with the poorly groomed!

From the Diary of America's Best Christian: The Price for Saving the
    Wrong People Is an Eternity of Annoyance   59

WWBR *who would betty rebuke?*

letting lesser ideologues know their place—hell

Betty Bowers Tells Laura Schlessinger: "I Say This with Much Christian Love,
    but You Are Simply Too Slutty to Speak at My Church, Dear"   63

WWBW *what would betty watch?*

hollywood trash so you don't have to—and then her perfect size 4 waist!

Betty's List of Movies with Acceptable Christian Messages   67
Betty's List of Forbidden Movies with Deplorable Messages   69
Roman Holler/Slay: Christian Persecution Is Back in Style in Hollywood!
    Betty Reviews the Film *Gladiator*   70
Betty's Exclusive Interview: Rapper Eminem Is Born Again!   73
From the Diary of America's Best Christian: Taking Time to Find the Sins
    More Careless Christians Overlook   77

WWBS *what would betty say?*

"you are going straight to hell"—and then an imprecatory prayer for your swift departure

Interview with Diane Sawyer   79
Epistle of Profound and Compassionate Christian Advice:
    School Prayer and Other Ways of Getting Back at Jews for Killing Jesus   82

HWBR *how would betty react?*

From the Diary of America's Best Christian: What to Do When
   Your Personal Savior Stops By Without Calling First   85

WWBG *where would betty go?*

to extremes to be america's most selfless christian—and then to her suite at the villa d'este on lake como for a month!

CHARITY: Surprising Those Who Think They Have Everything with
   Charming Gifts of the Holy Spirit   87
Epistle of Profound and Compassionate Christian Advice:
   Why Was Jesus Born in a Place Without Air-conditioning?   89

HWBM *how would betty mother?*

don't brag about your conception if your christian home is not also immaculate!

Sometimes a "Distant Father" Is Not Such a Bad Thing   91
Raising Cain: Earth's First Halfhearted Attempt at Parenting   92
In Biblical Times, the Desire to "Leave a Good Impression"
   Was Not Meant Metaphorically   93
Epistle of Profound and Compassionate Christian Advice:
   Does God Watch Us Masturbate?   94
America's First Lady Sits Down for a Lovely Chat About Family and
   Fashion with America's Best Christian   95
Pews News: Betty Performs Amalfi Coast Miracle After a Lovely Lunch   99
Epistle of Profound and Compassionate Christian Advice:
   Spare a Heavy Bible, Spoil the Child   100
Betty's Guide to Christlike Family Values   101
Epistle of Profound and Compassionate Christian Advice:
   An Open Mind Is the Devil's Playground   104
Betty's World-Famous "Brutal Death of Our Savior" Cookie Recipe   107

WWBW *what would betty wear?*

a look of humble self-sacrifice—and an $8,000 prada jacket!

Epistle of Profound and Compassionate Christian Advice:
    Wearing Execution Devices as Jewelry 109

Protect the Environment from Visual Pollution:
    Encourage the Poorly Dressed to Stay Home 111

Epistle of Profound and Compassionate Christian Advice:
    What Should a Christian Lady Wear to an Abortion-Clinic Bombing? 112

A Day in the Life of America's Best Christian:
    Knowing Which Designers and Heel Size Are Most Pleasing to the Lord 114

Epistle of Profound and Compassionate Christian Advice:
    What Does a Christian Lady Wear to a Stylish Execution? 115

From the Diary of America's Best Christian:
    Speaking in Tongues Without a TelePrompTer 118

WWBC *what would betty change?*

homosexuals—and then into something shimmering for dinner!

Baptists Are Saving Homosexuals:
    The World's Only Fortune 500 Ex-Gay Ministry 119

BASH Ex-Gay Testimony: Jesus Gave Me the One Thing I Always Lacked:
    Cachet! 120

The Homosexual Agenda Revealed! 121

Epistle of Profound and Compassionate Christian Advice:
    One Boy Scout Merit Badge Too Far 125

A Day in the Life of America's Best Christian:
    Cashing in Your Three-Dollar Bills 126

Epistle of Profound and Compassionate Christian Advice:
    Does an Ex-Gay Have to Give Up the Fabulous Gay Clothes? 128

Did Your Child Wake Up This Morning and Decide to Be a Homosexual? 130

W W B S *what would betty shoot?*

a look of unveiled reproof—and then a well-placed warning shot!

Pews News: Unarmed Student Shot in the Head by a Jesus Puppet   133

W W B A *what would betty avoid?*

giving in to sin—and then detection of her failure to do so!

Labels Are Not Just for Garments—Inspect All of Them!   135

How to Spot a Counterfeit Christian™   136

W W B T *what would betty teach?*

the importance of forgiveness—and then sinners a lesson!

Pews News: Creation Scientists Prove That Circles Are of Satan   139

H W B V *how would betty vote?*

republican—and repeatedly

Nonpartisan Christian Coalition Voter Guide   141

America's Best Christian: Spiritual Adviser to America's
    First Dysfunctional Family   143

W W B P *what would betty pack?*

three outfits a day—and then some heat!

What Every Saved Woman Should Have in Her Purse in Case of Rapture   149

 *what will betty do?*

How to Succeed at the Expense of Others in the Afterlife   153

Betty's Exclusive Interview with the Blessed Virgin   155

 *how will betty conclude?*

From the Diary of America's Best Christian:

    Quality Time with Your Personal Savior   165

BTCG *betty's true christian*™ *glossary*

167

WWBD?

Meet the Author

Some well-meaning, but nevertheless annoying, acquaintances have asked Mrs. Bowers if it is perhaps immodest to acknowledge that she is, by all credible accounts, America's best Christian. With sincerity worthy of Diana Ross, she smiles and patiently informs them that as she is actually the *world's* best Christian, touting herself as deserving that simple superlative in merely one country, albeit the only country that matters, seems rather modest indeed. Further, it is not as if she crowned herself with this rather obvious honor. Betty was awarded the title America's Best Christian by W.W.J.D. Power and Associates several years ago when they determined that she handily outperformed all other Christians in a nationwide study in the key areas that drive the Lord's satisfaction.

"Since I was created in God's image, if I don't look good, *He* doesn't look good."

Before she embarked on her rewarding career as a professional Christian, Mrs. Bowers had been Atlanta's most successful Realtor. After many lucrative years of showing multimillion-dollar mansions in the dogwood-speckled glens of Buckhead, Mrs. Bowers decided that she would rather live in opulence, instead of making it available to those less deserving. As Mrs. Bowers recounts, "God called me out of pandering to the needs of the inexplicably wealthy and promised that if I devoted my fabulous business instincts to Him, I would one day never have to share a formal, Italianate living room, much less a German SUV, with someone more wealthy than I. While the Lord routinely observes that the poor will always be with us, He has been rather emphatic that I needn't be one of them."

As Mrs. Bowers finds that she can seldom say no to the Lord, she immediately turned her entrepreneurial skills to establishing her first spiritual enterprise, Betty Bowers' Christian Crack Whore Ministry, LLC. "As soon as I

15

realized how much cash these industrious little harlots were dealing in, it wasn't long before I introduced them to the one thing that every Baptist knows will save even the most sullied soul—tithing." Betty Bowers' Christian Crack Whore Ministry, LLC, was an instant success. Last year, the ministry made its initial public offering, netting its proud founder over $200,000,000—God's way of showing His approval for Mrs. Bowers' selfless work to help the less fortunate. When asked by *The Wall Street Journal* to confirm this amount, Mrs. Bowers demurred: "I never discuss figures—except to say that I am still a perfect size four."

Introduction

FROM THE LOUIS QUINZE DESK OF

Betty Bowers

AMERICA'S BEST CHRISTIAN

Being asked by the secular publishing world to reveal my secrets of how I became America's best, most glamorous Christian is not something I regard with unqualified enthusiasm. Yes, there is the satisfaction of reminding people that, come Judgment Day, I will be whisked through the "Ten Sins or Less" express line while they are subjected to the ineptitude of surly seraphim and processing delays unfamiliar to those who have not tried to secure concert seats through Ticketmaster's 1-800 number. While, as a True Christian™, I believe that helping others is almost as important as a crisp hemline, I am left to ask the question that proves decisive for all who embark on a journey of profound spiritual meaning: What's in it for me? Do I really wish to open the door to Heaven for people I would not even choose to have in my lovely Christian home? After all, it is hard enough to avoid the truly dreadful here on Earth when they have only a finite amount of time to find you. And in Heaven you will be up against people cagey enough to have worked out which sins really matter and which can be ignored with impunity.

Every day, thousands of lost souls make a pilgrimage to my glorious website "Betty Bowers Is a Better Christian Than You!" (www.bettybowers. com). Its inspirational pages bring even the most worthless people from every corner of the Lord's Earth the good news that they are going straight to Hell. I have therefore undertaken to write this book, hoping to reverse the direction of their afterlife voyage and to indulge my acolytes' wistful quest to be just like me. After all, when it comes right down to it, ascension into Heaven is the only upward mobility that ultimately matters.

While it is ludicrous to assume that other, lesser people could ever replicate with any verisimilitude my finely calibrated knack for spotting a heretofore unnamed sin, to say nothing of the panache with which I carry off an edgy hat, this book will at least provide a voyeuristic peek into my world of social and spiritual preeminence. Whereas Stanislavsky offered a method for acting more like real people, I offer a method for acting better than real people. And my "method" is rather simple. If my acolytes merely ask themselves the simple question "What would Betty do?" when faced with any moral quandary—or simply two fabric swatches that both appear suitable—then they will find that not only will people instantly become more envious of them in this life, they may actually qualify to join me (though certainly not with any regularity) in the next.

The glorious day will soon arrive when people all across this once tasteful nation will not be able to buy a pack of mints, settle an argument, or choose a gasoline, much less a Personal Savior, without asking themselves, "What would Betty do?"

So close to Jesus, He validates my parking,

Betty Bowers

WWBH?

What Would Betty Have?

the appearance of absolute marital submission—and then her own way!

bringing integrity to christian homemakers

BITCH

Bringing Integrity To Christian Homemakers is a Baptist ladies' service organization that strives to keep Bible-based conversation to a maximum and recreational sex and frozen foods to a minimum in Christian, professionally decorated homes throughout God's country, America.

He has risen!—A born-again baking tip: While the Almighty can effortlessly expand a universe like a first-rate soufflé, He just can't seem to get the hang of basic baking. For example, the Lord told Ezekiel His secret for making a perfect barley cake—bake it with human dung (Ezekiel 4:12). I can't imagine what kitchen mishap caused our Lord to stumble upon this questionable technique, but it is safe to assume that there are no health inspectors in Heaven. Frankly, even though I am not quite sure what mesquite is, I am comforted by being fairly confident that I know from where it is not extruded.

from the diary of america's best christian: *protecting yourself from celestial voyeurs*

5:45 A.M., Bowers manse, Atlanta

As I emerged from a lovely Terme di Montecatini bath, I quickly covered myself with a bathrobe. A Christian lady should never become so preoccupied with her toilette that she forgets that sexual perverts might be in Heaven leering. Some lesser Christians forget that God's Glory is full of disreputable and vulgar apparitions. I am constantly reminding my acolytes that to get past the Lord's lax discretionary door,

So close to Jesus, we jog on Lake Como together.

all anyone has to do is simply to remember to accept Jesus as their Personal Savior moments before dying. As a result of this ill-conceived admittance policy, Heaven is absolutely overrun by dreadful people whose only virtue is a good sense of timing.

While I was thanking the Lord in front of my vanity mirror for His loving attention to detail, my assistant Miss Anne Thrope called to remind me of a breakfast engagement. Friend-of-Our-Lord Jerry Falwell was apparently scheduled to present me with an award from Bringing Integrity To Christian Homemakers at the Piedmont Driving Club. While I never expressly covet acclaim in an obvious manner, I never shirk duty—or the receipt of a well-deserved honor. So, without complaint, I would accept the lovely "Biggest B.I.T.C.H. in North America" Steuben crystal plaque. This citation is awarded annually to the president of the Bringing Integrity To Christian Homemakers chapter that has added the most paid members in the past year. I have won the title "Biggest B.I.T.C.H. in North America" on countless occasions. Indeed, I think I have, through the grace of God and somewhat arcane voting procedures, all but monopolized that honor. This year would, of course, be no exception. The Lord is, truly, so good to us!

B.I.T.C.H. submission muzzles have arrived just in time for this sunday's services!

"Let the woman learn in silence with all subjection. But I suffer not a woman to teach, nor to usurp authority over the man, but to be in silence."

I Timothy 2:11–12

In other words, God has made it quite clear that He will not countenance yammering by Christian women. And as Fundamentalist Christians, we obviously must obey the clear directives of our Lord, no matter how seemingly sexist. But let's be honest, gals. How many of us are godly enough to keep quiet in church—especially when Dora Denkins traipses down the aisle, late for service, reeking of stale tequila and last night's man? Nevertheless, we must do as the Lord commands and simply shut up! Because, like Eve before us, too many women are using their "free will" to disobey our Blessed Lord's annoyingly killjoy demands.

To help these sinning chatterboxes who obviously won't help themselves, Bringing Integrity To Christian Homemakers is introducing new designer B.I.T.C.H. submission muzzles. Starting next week, each wife will be given a submission muzzle with her hymnal when she enters Landover Baptist Church.

Mrs. Judy O'Christian of the Ladies of Landover, responding to the news, said, "We are all real excited about this. Besides, a Christian lady can never have enough accessories!" Unsaved Malaysian children will be working around the clock to ensure that there are enough muzzles by Sunday.

Obeying the Lord has never been more fashionable!

Sister Taffy demonstrates how the new imported Sunday service B.I.T.C.H. muzzles actually help to finish off a lovely outfit! You'll wonder how you got along without one.

Sometimes it is only my compassionate advice that stands between unsaved trash and the flames of Hell they so richly deserve.

epistle of profound and compassionate christian advice:
getting restraining orders against intrusive guardian angels

Dear Betty:

After spending a hellish day at the office, crawling through a rush-hour traffic jam, and coming home to find my condo in complete disarray, I strode into my bedroom to discover my husband engaged in an unseemly act of impurity with _my_ guardian angel! Fortunately, as a True Christian™, of course, I had a gun. I dashed to my dresser, pulled out my semiautomatic, and ordered that winged Jezebel out of my home! She dressed quickly and fluttered out the French window in a tizzy. But she wasn't nearly as upset as I was when I found the product of their seraphic love coil all over my limited edition Missoni bed sheets! I know that killing is sometimes wrong, and perhaps a futile gesture in this instance, but I want that celestial bitch to pay! What should I do?

Betrayed in Dallas

Dear Sinner Who Neglects Her Christian Home for Secular Work:

You have to understand that most guardian angels have endured fairly dull lives, dear. Living for someone else is never easy and seldom fulfilling. Just ask James Brolin. Guardian angels spend so much time in our Christian homes that they start acting as if they were invited guests. This is why I always warn my readers to look for signs that their guardian angel is getting a little too comfortable. Do you find your better perfume bottles suddenly half full or topped off with dewdrops? Is your angel unaccounted for at precisely the time you hear your Bentley pull out of the driveway on the way to an all-night "Put the Christ back in Xmas—Put the X back in Christ" rave? Do you find feathers in your underwear drawer? Is your vanity mirror always tilted toward the ceiling? Does your new silk dress bear imprints near the shoulders that suggest a gathering of poultry slipped it on and engaged in a vitriolic fight? If any of the aforementioned events occur unchecked, you are inviting a dangerous level of familiarity that will most certainly lead to contempt. Indeed, it is probably time to consult an attorney about a restraining order.

To my mind, having seraphim trail you 24-7 amounts to little more than supernatural stalking! My erstwhile guardian angel (a short woman who lived in Ecuador in the eighteenth century) spoke with such atrocious English that it became very frustrating even to pretend I was listening to such a poor, ignorant apparition. And she was constantly wearing a filthy bowler hat and a poncho with simply the most shocking juxtaposition of shrill colors—shades that didn't belong in the same time zone together! After several months of studiously ignoring her—and even taking the time to learn some Mexican so I could

say *"no más!"*—thinking she would take a hint, I had had quite enough.

I had her dismissed and never regretted that day. I am pleased to say that Jesus took my list of grievances about the woman so seriously that He immediately sent her hurtling straight toward Hell, where, no doubt, her indiscriminate style of dressing will go unnoticed. Since that dreadful experience, I have encouraged all who are having problems with meddlesome or annoying guardian angels similarly to dismiss these celestial interlopers. You will thank me.

So close to Jesus, He uses my birthday when He buys Lotto tickets,

Betty Bowers

P.S. When having guardian angels dismissed, it is wise to ensure that God demotes them to "demon" status, as it would be awkward to run into them in Heaven. No one wants to spend eternity with a disgruntled ex-employee.

"All the News That Fits, We Print"

New York End Times

The only newspaper in America that is "Untouched by Unsaved Hands"

Heaven: low 70, high 71
Hell: 4,323°
Outlook: bleak

Mrs. Betty Bowers Flies a Planeload of B.I.T.C.H.s to Italy

RAVELLO, ITALY. (AP) Last night, the annual Bringing Integrity To Christian Homemakers dinner was held at Betty Bowers' lovely eighteenth-century villa in Ravello, Italy. By all accounts, it was a huge success. All B.I.T.C.H. members and spouses who had tithed in excess of $144,000 (a dollar for each virgin man to ascend into Heaven per Revelation 14:3, verified as deposited in ready funds by Deutsche Bank Switzerland) during the past "spiritual" year were invited. These special contributors were driven by a fleet of white Rolls Silver Clouds chauffeured by "angels" to Landover Baptist Church's private tarmac to be flown to Italy in the Betty Bowers Christian Ministries' new custom "The Wings of Gabriel" Boeing 747–400. During the flight, catered by chef Jean-Georges Vongerichten, Barbra Streisand regaled the flock with impromptu banter read from cue cards between Baptist hymns. "She may be unsaved," noted Mrs. Bowers, "but she sounds like an angel and will sing anything if the price is right."

Once in Italy, the honored guests were whisked past the tawdry poverty of Naples onto the scenic coastal road that runs through Positano and down the Amalfi

Betty Bowers Christian Ministry "Wings of Gabriel" 747-400

Coast, providing breathtaking vistas to the fêted crowd. The highlight of the weekend was a sumptuous dinner at Mrs. Bowers' 7,600-square-foot home, Villa Cristo de Amalfi. "Roughly half the eligible Platinum tithers refused to attend," lamented Mrs. Bowers, stunning in a whimsical Comme des Garçons' Rei Kawakuba. "Since we are living in End Times, many True Christians are afraid of being caught overseas when the Lord comes in judgment. Frankly, nobody wanted to risk having to answer to a list of sins reeled off in a foreign language. I tried to explain that the Lord would just *know* they weren't Italian, but to no avail. In fairness to them, it is somewhat risky to be surrounded by Catholics when God is pointing fingers at who will go to Hell."

epistle of profound and compassionate christian advice:
salvation through skin care

While the focus-group-tested slogan "Love the sinner. Hate the sin" served us well during the past century, the new millennium calls for a fresh theological approach. That is why I have pioneered the more compassionate mantra: "Love the sinner. Hate their *clothes!*"

Dear Precious Sister-in-Christ Mrs. Bowers:

I am tired, Sister Betty. Sick and tired of defending the one, true Baptist faith to heathen women throughout Floyd County, Georgia. For years now, I have gone door to door, walking up on front porches and asking women to accept Jesus Christ as their Personal Savior. If they fall to their knees to accept their savior, I reward them with a free sample of Mary Kay lipstick or eye shadow (in a modest hue that is consistent with their new status as Baptists).

But there are so many of them, Betty. So many hell-bound Presbyterians and Seventh-Day Adventists and Methodists! When I come upon these harlots I ask them (right after I pretend to admire their country-casual decor): "And who did the Lord send to herald the birth of his son? Did he send . . . John the Catholic? Did he send . . . John the Mormon? Did he send . . . John the Whiskeypalian? No! No! No! The good Lord in His infinite wisdom sent a representative from His very own, hand-picked, preferred denomination, the Blessed Lord sent John the Baptist!" They never have a good response to that one.

Thank you, Sister Betty, for all your tireless efforts on behalf of tasteful, Baptist ladies. Please remember me in your prayers, and whenever you're running low on makeup. I have to pay a visit to a Catholic woman right now and talk about Christ and blueberry-sherbet eyeliner.

Yours dripping in the blood of the lamb (you should see my dry-cleaning bills!),

Mrs. Cooter Green

FROM THE LOUIS QUINZE DESK OF

Betty Bowers

AMERICA'S BEST CHRISTIAN

Dear Mrs. Green:

Thank you for your lovely letter and inspiring testimony, dear. My, what a difficult life you have chosen! Even a cursory look from a speeding car would reveal that the one thing Catholic women ignore more than their salvation is quality cosmetics. How wise of you to choose a product line that is crude enough to be almost accessible to lost harlots who have proven themselves to be rather ham-fisted with a tube of too-red lipstick. Do warn these women that once they have embraced the faith actually recognized by God (Baptist), they will have to forgo some of the more garish shades of eye shadow historically favored by Catholics and strippers. A saved woman's makeup should cover old sins, not entice new ones.

May I be so bold as to suggest that you reprioritize, dear? Instead of wasting your Christian charity getting these lost souls to become true Baptist Christians, and thereby eligible for Heaven, why not concentrate on their unfailingly wretched appearance first? After all, do we really want them to ascend to God's Glory still looking like Genoese wharf hookers? Surely, it would be in everyone's best interest to make sure Heaven is populated with Baptists who, through a rigorous regime of exfoliation, Retinol, and quality moisturizers, have saved their skin as well as their soul. Mary Kay is a lovely way for them to start without spending more money than they are, frankly, worth at this point. Once it looks as if they have accepted the true faith, it may be time to take them on a pilgrimage to a department store to pay homage at the pale green shrine to Estee Lauder.

So close to Jesus, we finish each other's sentences,

WWBR?

What Would Betty Read?

her autographed bible—and then her friends for their ill-conceived look!

epistle of profound and compassionate advice: *using the old testament to your advantage*

Dear Betty:

You say you are such a good Christian and yet you seem more like a Jew to me since you dwell so much on the Old Testament laws. Don't you know that Jesus freed us from those laws? Why do you constantly harp on them?

A Real Christian

FROM THE LOUIS QUINZE DESK OF

Betty Bowers

AMERICA'S BEST CHRISTIAN

Dear Deluded Sinner:

Contrary to your ridiculous statement, the Bible is rather accommodating in whether or not we True Christians™ are to follow the Old Testament. You see, Jesus said yes and Paul said no. Truly, it is a linguistic miracle that in providing for every conceivable contingency, the

So close to Jesus,

we have joint checking.

Lord's Word is not only inerrant, it is inerrant in several contradictory ways. So, you can choose which position suits you with impunity—and then change with neither notice nor reproach to suit your particular mood, need, or desired marital status.

While we True Christians™ claim that the Old Testament no longer binds us, this seems a rather rash position, given our fondness for the type of wrath and condemnation you simply can't find in the New Testament. Besides, Jesus was quite clearly in favor of kosher food and abridged penises. He said that the Old Laws would always be in place since "it is easier for Heaven and Earth to pass, than one tittle of the law to fail" (Luke 16:17). The best evidence we have that Jesus intended for Christians to observe Old Testament laws is to look at those closest to Him. Jesus' own brother James, who led the Jerusalem church, required new Christians to observe the Old Laws. Peter, the apostle Jesus selected to lead His church, was also under the impression that this is what Jesus had wished.

In contradistinction to the less-pragmatic Jesus, Paul was primarily interested in marketing our fabulous new religion to the Gentiles. Unfortunately, Corinthian focus groups were very negative when it was suggested that they think about having their penises gnawed at by what must have been, in Nothing A.D., fairly intimidating instrumentation. Being a rather resourceful marketing wiz, Paul responded by starting a glorious tradition that has gained great popularity with modern American Christians—he simply ignored Jesus.

Some may regard Paul's plan to throw out the Old Testament rather risky—especially since the new one had yet to be written, much less find a reputable publisher. Nevertheless, many of the Jewish laws are so onerous or annoying to neighbors (animal sacrifices come to mind) that even the Jews don't pay attention to them—so, truly, why should we be saddled with them? Besides, as a busy homemaker—since ignoring the Old Testament laws really cuts down on the pots and pans in the kitchen—I'm all for it!

So close to Jesus, I can flirt with Him and He knows it isn't going anywhere,

Betty Bowers

betty's handy true christian™ guide to biblical interpretation

Enjoy all of the piety of saying you follow the Bible—with none of the inconvenience of actually doing it!

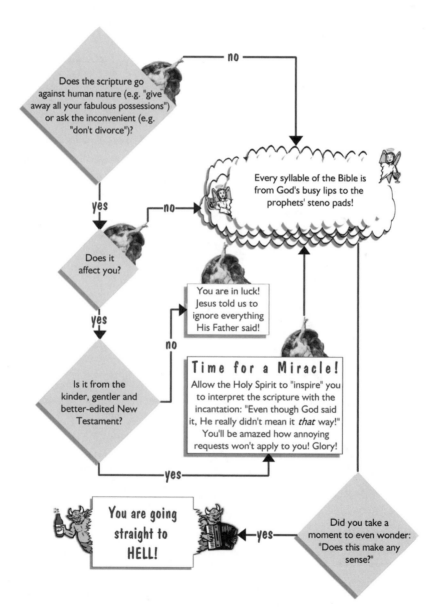

Does the scripture go against human nature (e.g. "give away all your fabulous possessions") or ask the inconvenient (e.g. "don't divorce")?

no

yes

Does it affect you?

no

yes

Is it from the kinder, gentler and better-edited New Testament?

no

Every syllable of the Bible is from God's busy lips to the prophets' steno pads!

You are in luck! Jesus told us to ignore everything His Father said!

Time for a Miracle! Allow the Holy Spirit to "inspire" you to interpret the scripture with the incantation: "Even though God said it, He really didn't mean it *that* way!" You'll be amazed how annoying requests won't apply to you! Glory!

yes

You are going straight to HELL!

yes

Did you take a moment to even wonder: "Does this make any sense?"

With several bottles of white-out and a long weekend, you'll be surprised how quickly you can make your Bible consistent with traditional family values!

epistle of profound and compassionate christian advice:
are you keeping track of how many times you are born again?

Dear Mrs. Bowers:
I don't understand the basic principles of your religion at all. For example, could you please explain the difference between a regular Christian and a born-again Christian?
Puzzled in Portland

FROM THE LOUIS QUINZE DESK OF
Betty Bowers
AMERICA'S BEST CHRISTIAN

Dear Ignorant Sinner:
The First Rule of Christianity is "All humans are worthless scum who should be tortured forever in Hell by the loving God who created them." Say that forty times when you wake up (preferably without makeup in front of a bathroom mirror, allowing you to empathize more with God's disgust). The Second Rule, which follows from the First, is that anything good that happens is because of God and anything bad that happens is because of *you.* Heaven, which God created? All the credit goes to God! Hell, which God created? All the blame goes to us! Are you following? Make sure you are, because the next part gets tricky.

The Third (and most important) Rule of Christianity is "Because God created people who disappointed Him so much, He committed suicide over them." Now, granted, some might regard this as a somewhat showy and unbalanced gesture for attention from Someone who knows He can't actually die, but that is why the Fourth Rule of Christianity is "It's not supposed to make sense." This is axiomatic with the Fifth Rule, "We are too stupid to understand God's reasons, but He will torture us in Hell for misconstruing His perfect, yet oblique, will." Now, the only way you can be spared from Hell is to accept Jesus as your Personal Savior, which is like having a personal shopper who dresses appallingly and won't go away when you say, "I'm just looking." What this means is that Jesus doesn't really care if you follow His Father's Old Testament rules, just as long as you keep telling Jesus how wonderful He is. Let's face it; we've all had friends like that.

Okay, now you understand what it takes to be a generic Christian, let me explain why some of us say we are "born-again Christians." Once was good; twice is better. Just look what it did for the twice-baked potato!

Some Fundamentalist Christians, far less devout than I, have been born again only once. While it is certainly admirable that these people, so otherwise halfhearted in their facsimile of faith, took the time to be born a second time, such a lackadaisical embrace of faith no longer qualifies one for entry by Heaven's discretionary door policy! I am now ready for that knowing nod from the burly doorman that will signal that I will be whisked past the less-born-again crowd, directly into God's VIC (Very Important Christian) lounge for complimentary refreshments! Indeed, as America's best Christian, I have been born again so often it took a team of accountants from Price Waterhouse Coopers four full days to audit my spiritual rebirths.

So close to Jesus, He is invading my personal space,

Betty Bowers

christian bs: bible study. the gospel according to mrs. betty bowers

And all the devils besought him, saying, Send us into the swine, that we may
enter into them. And forthwith Jesus gave them leave. And the unclean spirits
went out, and entered into the swine: and the herd ran violently down a steep
place into the sea, (they were about two thousand;)
and were choked in the sea.

Mark 5:12–13

This riveting passage of Mark recounts how a pleasantly spoken pack of demons asked Jesus if He would give them permission to set up living quarters in a herd of indolent pigs grazing on a mountainside. (Why pigs were gathered like a convention of goats, the good Lord chooses not to reveal—and I find it is usually best not to ask.) Perhaps recognizing that pigs on mountainsides would have fabulous views, Jesus quite graciously indulged the demons' wanderlust, allowing them to relocate into the swine. No sooner had the demons unpacked, two thousand pigs, apparently displeased with their new tenants, ran down the hill and jumped into the ocean to drown, instantly transforming the demons' accommodations from ocean-view to less-desirable ocean-*floor*-view rooms. What an odd spectacle! Had Jesus not been a Jew, I imagine He might have given more thought to what His casual decision had, no doubt, just done to the local price of pork.

WWBD?

What Won't Betty Do?

in her walk-in closet, anything twice—in her marital bedroom, anything once

saving love until the sacrament

Saving Love Until The Sacrament teaches young girls that if they make a mistake and allow a boy to go too far before marriage, God will torture them for eternity in Hell.

The message is clear: No sex before marriage and as little sex as they can get away with after marriage.

Next Week's Lecture: "The Only Thing You Should Cover with Plastic—Leftovers!"

Saving Love Until The Sacrament

Knees Together For Christ

is the bible too smutty for a christian home?

As is so often the case with rushed sequels, the New Testament lacks the quirky sense of high drama of the original installment. Despite its marvelously inventive plot twists, it is my considered opinion that certain portions of the Bible are simply too ribald for children and no more suitable in a Christian home than a copy of *Hustler*. As a concerned mother and founder of Bringing Integrity To Christian Homemakers, it would not behoove me to allow any smut into my Christian home—regardless of the author. And, frankly, one is hard pressed to find a book more salacious than the one written by the Blessed Lord, the Bible.

Look, for example, at the story of the resourceful widow Ruth. Naomi,

Ruth's mother-in-law, obviously quite the romantic, encouraged Ruth to perform oral sex on the floor of a grain warehouse with a rich old man called Boaz after he had boozed it up all evening. I don't know the Hebrew, but the English word for this is "pimping." In doing so, Naomi has much in common with a modern-day Naomi (Judd) who also uses the greater talents of a daughter to get ahead.

Ruth is all too typical of the loose-moraled sluts who fill the pages of the Bible. While both God and Jackie Collins apparently believe that the inclusion of mercenary harlots enhances the marketability of their books, I simply cannot recommend either author to Christian families concerned with the ethical upbringing of young ladies. Louisa May Alcott was able to tell a moral tale for girls without pandering to seamy sensationalism. Would that I could say the same for our Blessed Lord's literary efforts.

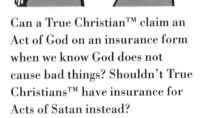

Can a True Christian™ claim an Act of God on an insurance form when we know God does not cause bad things? Shouldn't True Christians™ have insurance for Acts of Satan instead?

To protect my lovely Christian children from lurid and purely gratuitous tales of unwholesome carnality, I have, in consultation with my pastor at Landover Baptist Church, redacted all of the offending portions of the now Good Book. We, of course, started with the pornographic Song of Solomon. It was removed in its entirely after Pastor read it several times to be sure it was as filthy as it seemed. (He assured me that it was.)

This means that the Bowers' family Bible contains no scripture addressing *adultery* (Deuteronomy 28:30), *prostitution* (Deuteronomy 22:28, 29), *sexual mutilation* (I Samuel 18:25, 27), *exhibitionism and public sexual intercourse* (II Samuel 16:21, 22), *forced sexual slavery* (Deuteronomy 21:11, 13), *bestiality* (Leviticus 20:16), *rape and grotesque sex killings* (Judges 19:22, 29), *whoredom* (Ezekiel 23:2, 20), *sexually aggressive tramps* (Genesis 39:7, 12), *incestuous rape* (II Samuel 3:1, 14), *offering daughters to strangers as sexual door prizes* (Genesis 19:8), *drunken incest* (Genesis 19:31, 36), *multiple sex partners* (I Kings 11:1, 3), *infanticide and abortion* (Isaiah 13:16), (Ezekiel 9:6), (Psalms 137:8, 9), (Amos 1:13), (I Kings 15:16), *cannibalism* (Deuteronomy 28:53), and *masturbation and coitus interruptus* (Genesis 38:9)—just to name a few passages off the top of my head (I am too much of a lady even to allude to passages that relate to people eating their own feces!).

After numerous swipes with a big, black marker, the Bowers' family Bible Old Testament looks like a letter sent by a GI during WWII after the war censors got to it. Redacting all the smutty scriptures has allowed us to read the entire Old Testament in roughly three-quarters of the time it takes the other families on our street to read their disgusting, unchristian version. And this spiritual shortcut has allowed the Bowers family to read the Old Testament more often than any family I know, which means that we are, in turn, better Christians than any of our neighbors.

So close to Jesus,

He gave me His
loaves and fish recipe..

In short, if you seek risqué literary examples of how to draw attention to yourself, stick to Jacqueline Susann. Her heroines wear much nicer shoes and are less likely to be killed by hurled objects or turned into condiments, such as pillars of presumably kosher salt (Genesis 19:26). And speaking of Lot's wife, knowing what we do about her wretched husband and insouciant daughters (who got their father drunk and had sex with him—and these were the people from Sodom the Lord *spared*!), I can't help but think it must have been quite a relief to the woman when God gave her the opportunity to investigate the less morally ambiguous life enjoyed by most salts. While her doctor, no doubt, must have been alarmed by such high levels of sodium, salt's well-known inability to effectively communicate at least provided the poor woman a perfect excuse for avoiding the unpleasantness of having to explain to strangers that her stepchildren were also her grandchildren, which is probably never an easy concept to broach (Genesis 19:31–36).

Since my faith celebrates Someone who was tortured with nails and forced to drink vinegar, I view each gallery opening, with its domestic champagne and two hours in Gucci stilettos, as simply one more opportunity to be utterly Christlike.

god created adam and his wife, eve— not adam and his domestic partner, steve

As a True Christian™, I must take a moment to reject the secular heresy of so-called "evolution." My idea of natural selection is picking up a pair of Gucci sling backs at Barneys to complement my new Hermès silk suit. Sure, the idea that we are après apes is intriguing (and, in regard to some men, a transformation somewhat overstated), but can tedious biological permutations really hold a candle to a tawdry tale of naked people who lie, murder, and commit incest? I am, of course, talking about the delightful Adam and Eve clan.

We may not approve of Adam and Eve, but they happen to be God's models for the rest of us. So let's review the lessons that can be gleaned from their creation. As we know, God first formed man from dirt. Casual observation reveals that this easy recipe shows all signs of still working today with few, if any, additional ingredients. As America's most saved Baptist, I feel compelled to mention what the Lord did *not* create next. You will please note the absence of the famous-by-omission Steve, Adam's would-be gay fling. As we True Christians™ are wont to say, "God created Adam and Eve, not Adam and Steve."

I adore surprises. With two exceptions. A Christian lady should never be surprised after a hair appointment or Judgment Day.

Had he been created, Steve would have been the first human being to compare penis size and, no doubt, criticize the cut of Eve's hair and fig-leaf ensemble. Instead of creating a special friend for Adam, God gave him a woman, thus delaying the appalling advent of homosexuality by approximately twenty to thirty years.

biblically correct sexual survival tips

Onan, while having sex with his brother's wife (don't ask), ejaculated on the carpet. The Lord, being a somewhat anal deity, knew that even a dab of club soda wouldn't get that unsightly stain out and instantly killed Onan for his sloppy aim (Genesis 38:9–10). On the other hand, so to speak, the Lord knows that just a splash of water will get unsightly semen stains out of clothing and off of skin (Leviticus 15:17). (But not poly blends, as God, unbeknownst to most Evangelicals, has quite rightly forbidden blends, as they are an abomination) (Deuteronomy 22:11). If, however, you are sleeping with men who have penises the size of donkeys and ejaculations as profuse as horses (as was the case with the braggart Oholibah in Ezekiel 23:20), Mrs. Bowers recommends a touch of liquid detergent in the prewash.

SURVIVALTIP Out damned spot: When ejaculating, aim for your clothes or skin, but avoid the floor at all costs.

You are not to "lie with any beast" (Leviticus 18:23). I am uncertain if this pertains to prevaricating with livestock or was a prophecy intended solely for the benefit of Donald Trump's parade of myopic bimbos. In either case, I can hardly see any downside in adhering to God's wishes.

SURVIVALTIP The Lord is a little more persnickety than Jeanne-Marie LePrince de Beaumont when it comes to dating: no beasts—no exceptions!

If you are killing people you don't like and see someone beautiful, feel free to take her home with you and shave all her hair off and clip her nails. But wait at least a month before "going into her" (Deuteronomy 21:11–14). Presumably, this waiting period before sex is to allow the erstwhile beautiful woman to get used to her new involuntary punk look. No woman wants to have sex when she feels unattractive.

SURVIVALTIP If you kidnap a beautiful woman for sex, surprise her with an outré-chic "prisoner of war" makeover.

"Thou shalt not lie with mankind, as with womankind: it is abomination" (Leviticus 18:22). While many faux-Christians interpret this to mean men should not have sex with other men, the Holy Spirit has led me to read this as a proscription against men having sex with men "as with" a woman. This is God's way of suggesting that men should, in contradistinction to how they treat women, try to think of the other man's feelings and, for instance, call the next day (and not at a time when they are sure they will just get voice mail). For, truly, the way men sleep with women is an abomination.

SURVIVALTIP When a man has sex with another man, flowers the next day are never remiss.

King David bought his wife with 200 Philistine foreskins (I Samuel 18:25). A modern bride is best to stipulate that dowry jewels do not include so-called "family jewels."

SURVIVALTIP When listing wedding presents at department stores, try to be specific in your requests.

King David told his special friend Jonathan: "I am distressed for thee, my brother Jonathan: very pleasant hast thou been unto me: thy love to me was wonderful, passing the love of women" (II Samuel 1:26). Considering just how many concubines and wives David had loved, this is high praise indeed to the, no doubt, exhausted Jonathan.

SURVIVALTIP When a man with numerous lovers and ten concubines says you are good, chances are he knows what he is talking about.

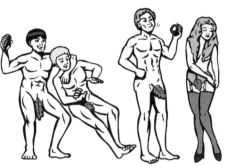

an apple was not the only forbidden thing the trollop eve put in her mouth: the sexual escapades of this planet's first family

I am well aware that Adam and Eve's family were a first attempt at creating humans, but it would be difficult to conjure such a mélange of dysfunctionality, gratuitous melodrama, and nonsensical plot twists outside of a Tori Spelling movie of the week. Between us, I secretly cherish the wistful notion that ours was merely a practice universe. A cosmic mulligan, if you will. To think otherwise hardly speaks well of the Almighty's ability to create anything either charming or useful.

Nevertheless, we are stuck with Adam and Eve and will simply have to resign ourselves to making sense of their tawdry tale. I must caution my fellow Christians that using the Adam and Eve family as a paradigm of God's plan for your own family is fraught with dicey messages and potentially treacherous bedroom diplomacy. While I believe that Christian families should be close, I prefer to observe a few limitations on familial familiarity. Not so for our Lord. For example, it appears that it was God's plan that in order to populate our lovely planet, sons should sleep with either their mother or sisters. After all, God created only one man and one woman, not an entire subdivision. So how did they get grandchildren? Well, I am too much of a Christian lady to spell it out for you, but you can do the math. Let's just say that it is alarmingly evident that Eve made quite a habit out of sticking forbidden things in her!

Further, why did God initially give Adam and Eve two boys if His plan was to procreate by having a romp with your sibling? I can only imagine that the Lord realized this oversight after twenty or so years. The problem was then remedied—as were most tricky situations in the Old Testament—by killing. Once Abel was out of the way, Cain was free to sleep with Mom or his much, much younger sisters. So, at a minimum, the male fondness for sexual relations with either the young or the illicit were established by this planet's second generation. On a more pleasant note, with people living to the hoary age of 969 (Genesis 5:27), the possibility of having sex with someone *fifty* times your age makes some of the ingénue-geriatric romantic matchups in Hollywood's films seem almost bearable to contemplate by comparison.

41

epistle of profound and compassionate christian advice:
whom did mary have sex with?

The Bible says it; I'll believe anything, and that settles it!

Dear Mrs. Bowers:

I'm very concerned about something I thought while reading my Bible. I asked my mother about it, but she just looked like she always does when Daddy asks her what happened to his Xanax. Then she told me to stop thinking so much. So I thought I would ask you since you are our country's greatest Christian. If God = Jesus = Holy Spirit, and Mary was impregnated by the Holy Spirit, didn't she have sex with her son?

Yours truly,

John, age 11

FROM THE LOUIS QUINZE DESK OF

Betty Bowers

AMERICA'S BEST CHRISTIAN

Dear Inquisitive Sinner,

I must commend your mother for not even trying to answer your impertinent inquiry. She, no doubt, knows that a razor-sharp eye for details and discrepancies is to be eschewed when it comes to studying God's inerrant Word. After all, when Christianity went through a period known as the "Inquisition," it was not laypeople asking the questions, dear. Remember that. When reading the Bible, even to mutter "why?"

is tantamount to sending up an enormous smoke signal to Satan: "Come and poison my malleable little mind with a distaste for the non-sensical!" In the future, if you find yourself involuntarily resorting to trying to make sense of what you read in the Bible, you may wish to mimic your mother's sound approach and simply find out where your father keeps his Xanax, dear.

So close to Jesus, I wear safety goggles to protect my eyes from the thorns,

Betty Bowers

betty's ex cathedra encyclical on same-sex marriage

I have long been an outspoken advocate in favor of so-called "same-sex" marriages. Indeed, I am constantly beseeching couples at our Bringing Integrity To Christian Homemakers' married couples ministry to abandon the amorally hedonistic notion that spouses must come up with a new "position" every six weeks when they have sex. Changes in position are best left to politicians. It is far easier to schedule an appropriate amount of time for necessary sexual congress when a couple simply has the same sex every time. If you want unpleasant surprises, befriend Patsy Ramsey, but the marital bedroom should be a place of utter darkness where the most unsavory of all connubial duties—godly submission to an ungodly act—can be performed in such a manner that the wife's involvement is not so strenuous that she loses her place in the Lord's Prayer.

> **Christian Hostess Tip:** When parents kill an insolent child, the Bible reminds us that it is polite to invite the neighbors to join in the stoning. While it might seem a gruesome pretext for getting to know the people next door, you must remember that parents in biblical times did not otherwise have the opportunity to gather around their children and hurl invective, as it was many centuries before the advent of Little League.

As I told a rather annoying Québecois official while visiting that dreadful cold country to the north (pointedly in English): "Do you remember the story of the tower of Babel, dear? God felt threatened by how well people were working together, so He made them all speak gibberish so that the building was never completed and the developer lost all his pre-leases. People speaking different languages was God's idea of punishment, dear, not a game plan. If you want diversity, try dressing in mixed patterns."

when it comes to sex, a baptist lady never does anything that

✟ involves special ordering.

✟ will turn her wig more than 15 degrees in either direction.

✟ she wouldn't mind her dear departed parents in Heaven grabbing popcorn and watching.

✟ requires her to shave above the knee.

✟ would suggest to her husband that she is actually enjoying herself unless, as is often the case, this will only serve to cause her husband to lose interest and stop.

✟ would leave toe prints on the headboard.

✟ causes her to perspire.

✟ obliterates the crisp crease in her 400-plus thread count "Shroud of Turin" pattern "Exodus from Egyptian Cotton" sheets upon completion of her onerous marital duties.

✟ involves any animal noises not made by an actual household pet, which at all times will keep at least two paws on the bedroom floor.

✟ appears in the Old Testament.

✟ will leave lipstick on any body part not seen in church.

✟ involves participation in a "Trinity."

✟ requires placing any body part in her mouth—unless, of course, it is the Body of Christ.

WWBH?

Who Would Betty Help?

not the so-called homeless—but herself to another beluga toast point!

CHARITY: sometimes jesus calls upon us to acknowledge even the truly dreadful

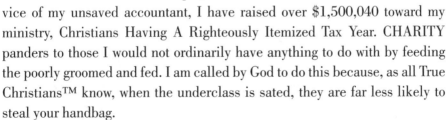

As most informed Christians know, the good Lord changed the rules for salvation to exclude good works simply to accommodate my busy schedule. This indulgence hasn't, however, stopped me from effortlessly setting the type of saintly example that puts other, lesser Christians to shame. For example, on the advice of my unsaved accountant, I have raised over $1,500,040 toward my ministry, Christians Having A Righteously Itemized Tax Year. CHARITY panders to those I would not ordinarily have anything to do with by feeding the poorly groomed and fed. I am called by God to do this because, as all True Christians™ know, when the underclass is sated, they are far less likely to steal your handbag.

As a New Millennium Republican who has embraced the mantra of "compassionate conservatism," I would rather someone flirt with starvation than risk reliance on my money. That is why CHARITY offers college-credit "begging workshops" to help poor pathetic creatures learn to be more productive in their chosen entrepreneurial vocation as panhandlers. After all, the more productive they are in securing financing from gullible pedestrians, the more likely it is that they will tithe—thus ensuring their salvation.

from the diary of america's best christian: *finding starvation's silver lining*

8:47 P.M., Kenya, Africa

This morning, while doing selfless missionary work, the Lord blessed me. I purchased a fabulous *méridienne* from a family in the village that was down on its collective heels. The piece is sublime, but the circumstances surrounding its purchase were almost sad. The family's home looked lovely from the road, but as my Range Rover approached its exhausted veranda, it was clear that only shy hints remained of the building's European-style grandeur. The building dated back to the halcyon days of English colonial times in Kenya when locals wielded croquet mallets instead of shotguns. Honestly, those Africans didn't know when they had a good thing. Try getting a truly dry martini, much less a pressed white tablecloth, at any restaurant in the Kenyan countryside now!

When I passed the muddy threshold, the home looked more decayed inside than even its shrugging roofline suggested. I was reminded of a particularly egregious "before" segment of a home-renovating program on PBS. You know, the one where you think, They will never do *anything* to make that dreadful oak billiard room work! The hand-painted Chinese wallpaper was peeling so much at the seams that it gave the disconcerting appearance of being a repeating pattern. The Aubusson rug was worn to the thickness of stubbly access-road-motel towels. Its delicate patterns were obscured by umber splotches and ragged holes. Truly, in times of famine, nuances of Christian housekeeping seem to be the first thing to go.

The purpose of my visit to this once lovely home was to bring rice for the family's starving children before rushing off to a fabulous indigenous luncheon with fellow mis-

So close to Jesus, He turns a deaf ear to the prayers of people who snub me at parties.

sionary Sister Taffy. As America's most saved Baptist, I adore helping others even though I expect no more than the usual thanks. Besides, I am scheduled to speak with Katie Couric when I return to air-conditioning, and I really need a charming anecdote about my charity in case someone from the IRS is watching. As soon as I walked into a room the family passed off as a parlor, I saw the settee. I immediately knew that it was absolutely priceless and I had to have it. Isn't it funny how you see something totally reupholstered in your mind's eye and just know it will be perfect in a setting away from other people's lackluster decorating? The Lord blesses some of us with such marvelous gifts!

I quite skillfully negotiated with the family to give me the Napoleonic piece for three and one-half bags of rice. I was willing to go as high as eighty bags, so I couldn't believe my good fortune when they came down from their original counteroffer of six. Truly, I've found that in places of abject hunger, you can pick up the loveliest pieces for little more than a packet of Life Savers. And to think I had initially been reluctant about going to Africa as part of my annual CHARITY mission! The settee is proof positive that God truly does reward those who think of others.

Biblical Shopping Tip: As it says in Deuteronomy 22:12, "Thou shalt make thee fringes upon the four quarters of thy vesture, wherewith thou coverest thyself." God, like Dale Evans, is mad about fringe!

the poor will always be with us, so we needn't break a heel rushing to help them

The Devil's greatest weapons are reason and investment property. It is far more dangerous to give in to the former.

Dearest Sister Betty:

This morning as I settled into the comfort of my four-seasons observatory, there were the usual letters and postcards from Christian (Baptist) friends. One item of mail, however, struck me as very peculiar. It was a glossy brochure with a picture of past Demon-crat President Jimmy Carter wearing coveralls and holding a shovel in his hand. Well, I must admit I was intrigued to see exactly what a tree-hugging liberal thinks that he could say that would interest me. Perhaps he had been placed in a work camp for ruining our economy and was sending out a letter of apology to all decent hardworking Republican Americans.

When I looked inside, I almost fell out of my chair. This was not an apology! This was a pledge form asking ME for money to help build homes for those lazy homeless people. Jesus immediately led me to the appropriate scripture: "He that buildeth his house with other men's money is like one that gathereth himself stones for the tomb of his burial." (Although I was surprised to note that He is familiar with Apocrypha!)

In other words, people who accept free homes from so-called Christians are building their own graves and are going to HELL. And weak-kneed liberals who donate money and labor to this "Habitat for Homeless Degenerates" are just doing the Devil's works. Yes they are.

Yours in Christ,
Sister Taffy

Dearest Sister Taffy:

Your righteous Christian disgust is quite justified. What an outrageous waste of time and money it is to be putting a roof over the unsaved! This is money that could be better spent converting Christian broadcasting stations throughout the land to high-definition TV standards. Our Blessed Savior lamented that the poor would always be with us, but He certainly said nothing about building them a pied-à-terre.

Of course, liberals have willfully misconstrued our Blessed Savior's passing suggestion about helping the poor. During His day, before diversified portfolios and a stock market that gets higher than Robert Downey, Jr., it was not a particularly onerous request of His followers to give away their few possessions to the poor—they *were* the poor! Let's face it, none of His disciples had a summer home on the Dead Sea. Nowadays, Christ wouldn't dream of making such a Marxist suggestion to his now more affluent followers.

Besides, after many hours with my Bible and unsaved tax accountant, I have come to the epiphany that Jesus never meant for us to give anything to the poor *now*. He meant, of course, to do it after we are called to God's Glory! You see, He is very clear in letting us know that the meek shall inherit the Earth. And, frankly, they will be welcome to it, as the rest of us will have moved to our fabulously well-appointed mansions in the sky by then.

Don't you see how our Lord's request that we give to the poor makes perfect sense? We can now all go out shopping for ourselves, sanguine in the knowledge that we have already purchased everything we own for the poor—as they will inherit every bit of it when we are called to Heaven! And, let's face it, who would want a drafty little clapboard shotgun, thrown together by accountants and bearing no architectural

flourish, when one can simply wait until the Rapture and move into my lovely twenty-three-room Manhattan co-op or Atlanta manse? See how generously we Christians provide for the less fortunate? Enough is enough!

So close to Jesus, He's seen me without makeup (once),

Betty Bowers

Every Knee
Shall Bend

BETTY BOWERS'

Christian

Crack Whore

Ministry

"Girls, if you are going to be down on your knees 14 to 37 times a night, you may as well pray while you are down there!"

-- Betty Bowers

What Would Betty Throw?

a soirée and then a few stones!

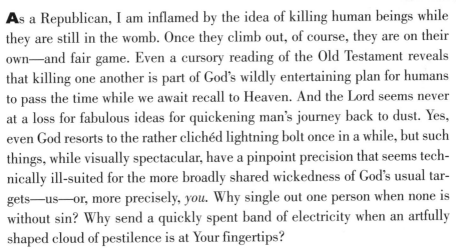

DEATH ROW BEAUTY TIP: When you shower on the day you are to be executed, don't forget to use an extra dab of quality conditioner. That way, you can take advantage of the extra body that electrocution gives an otherwise lifeless coif without suffering the embarrassment of spending your last few moments in public with flyaway hair.

As a Republican, I am inflamed by the idea of killing human beings while they are still in the womb. Once they climb out, of course, they are on their own—and fair game. Even a cursory reading of the Old Testament reveals that killing one another is part of God's wildly entertaining plan for humans to pass the time while we await recall to Heaven. And the Lord seems never at a loss for fabulous ideas for quickening man's journey back to dust. Yes, even God resorts to the rather clichéd lightning bolt once in a while, but such things, while visually spectacular, have a pinpoint precision that seems technically ill-suited for the more broadly shared wickedness of God's usual targets—us—or, more precisely, *you*. Why single out one person when none is without sin? Why send a quickly spent band of electricity when an artfully shaped cloud of pestilence is at Your fingertips?

SURVIVALTIP Some may scoff at the idea of killing, but if it is done for retribution or fur, I'm all for it.

---

imaginative ways the lord has killed or otherwise inconvenienced people

When the Lord tells us "Vengeance is mine" (Romans 12:19), He isn't succumbing to hollow boasting. In comparison to our Lord's resourceful repertoire of ways to ensure demise, even Jeffrey Dahmer comes off as rather milquetoast and squeamish. Indeed, compared to what usually befell sinners in the Old Testament, lethal injections strike me as nothing short of mollycoddling felons! To remind the occupants of death row just how easy they have it, I have prepared the following list they can tape above their bunk beds (which they can casually peruse while submitting to unholy acts in exchange for a pack of unfiltered cigarettes):

So close to Jesus,

I've had to get a restraining order (twice).

✝ God burns to death people who complain (Numbers 11:1). No one can fault God for hating whiners. I only wish He were more vigilant in His enforcement today!

✝ When people rub God the wrong way, He kills them with a series of calamities. The merciful Lord burns people, then shoots them with arrows, then makes them hungry, burns them again for good measure, then sends beasts to gnaw on them, then poisonous snakes, and then with a sword on their outside and terror on their inside (which I would think, considering the circumstances, would be a given), He finishes them off (Deuteronomy 32:21–25)! As you can see, the Almighty is not one to send mixed signals—well, except for the Old and New Testaments, of course.

✝ The Lord inflicts those who annoy Him with embarrassing hemorrhoids (I Samuel 5:9). With this in mind, I have found that one chummy conversation over cocktails with my local pharmacist reveals more about who in our community is displeasing to the Lord than even reading their mail.

✞ If you forget God, He will tear you to pieces (Psalms 50:22). This is a rather disconcerting way to go since you will have no idea who is killing you. My suggestion: Tie a string around your finger—unless, of course, God has already given you leprosy (II Kings 15:5).

GOD'S WRATH

✞ The Lord tells us that "happy is he who smashes the heads of little children on rocks" (Psalms 137:9). Well, to each his own, I guess, but I have always rather preferred a quiet game of bridge after dinner.

✞ If you mock your father or disobey your mother, the ravens will pick out your eyeballs and feed them to the eagles (Proverbs 30:17). Sharper than a serpent's tooth may be an ungrateful child, but clearly ravens are more than up to the task when it comes to payback.

✞ When the mood strikes Him, the Almighty commands friends to eat each other (Jeremiah 19:7–9). A rather poor translation of this verse was behind some shocking sexual shenanigans in Pentecostal circles in the early 1970s.

✞ "The people of Samaria must bear their guilt, because they have rebelled against their God. They will fall by the sword; their little ones will be dashed to the ground; their pregnant women ripped open" (Hosea 13:16). As a Republican, I hasten to remind my readers that this does not make God technically "pro-choice" since the woman involved is not given any say-so in her own death, much less that of the child. If any exception to the Almighty's otherwise unflinching adherence to the God's Own Party platform can be inferred, it is that the Lord is in favor of abortion only when the life of the mother is at stake (that is, when there is fear that she might actually live).

✞ The angel of the Lord killed Herod by having him "eaten by worms" because "he gave not God the glory" (Acts 12:23). I find it a good rule of thumb to give the Lord whatever He asks for—except investment advice.

✝ When forty-two little children make fun of a bald man, God sends bears to maul them to death (II Kings 2:23–24). God does not say if He was one of these bears, but He does elsewhere acknowledge that He is wont to kill people "like a bear robbed of her cubs" (Hosea 13:8). Some might suggest that the Lord's response to impolite comments about personal appearance was a bit overwrought, but it is my understanding that God has yet to recover from some fairly unkind remarks made by Moses when the Lord flashed His backside to the otherwise tactful prophet. ("And I will take away mine hand, and thou shalt see my back parts" [Exodus 33:23].)

✝ If you sell land and sneakily hold back some of the money (say, to buy a meal) from God, He will strike you dead immediately (Acts 5:1–10). Hire a Realtor. They are much more experienced at lying than you are.

SURVIVALTIP People who complain about the quality of the bread they are served get fiery serpents to bite them to death (Numbers 21:5–6). Remember that when the waitress asks you if everything is all right next time you eat at the Olive Garden.

---

having the honor of casting the first stone

While it is important for communities to rally together and participate in physical exercise, public stonings strike me as rather gruesome civic activities. Nevertheless, it is obviously something God is rather keen on, so it is hardly my place to turn my nose up at an opportunity to pelt someone with a sharp piece of anthracite. Jesus Himself stated that she who is without sin should have the honor of casting the first stone. This distinction is very much akin to the American tradition of asking a noted politician or celebrity to throw out the first ball of the baseball season. If you are going to go to all the trouble of being sinless, Jesus wanted to make sure that you had some earthly reward for your efforts.

Jesus said, "Let she who is without sin cast the first stone." That would be me.

SURVIVALTIP When engaging in even light stoning, a Christian lady always wears gloves. It is one thing for secular people to find you callous; it is quite another for them to find you have callused a finger.

Once the honorary first stone has been cast, according to Jesus, it then becomes open season for even the most spiritually besmirched to join in on the fun. This is why, in spite of the amazing accuracy of my lobs, I try to avoid a fatal blow (as a Christian, one should try occasionally to think of others)— unless the accused has slighted me at a cocktail party.

state executions: america's timid replication of old testament wrath

God's mandated stonings are still the benchmark by which all later methods of ganging up on and brutally killing someone are compared. While we True Christians™ try to carry on God's penchant for a grisly demise, we find ourselves annoyingly restrained by criminal laws and dry-cleaning bills (even God gets difficult-to-remove bloodstains on His casual wear! [Isaiah 63:3]). Take, for example, the rather pallid enterprise of state executions. Nowadays, those who take the trouble to attend an execution are left to mutely watch, denied the exhilaration of hurling either invective or granite. While undoubtedly satisfying, these regimented deaths have none of the spontaneity of an Old Testament stoning.

The less-participatory nature of modern killings does not, however, mean that those attending should shirk their duty to add ritualistic flair. For example, my chapter of Right to Life tries to have a celebratory execution tailgate party in the prison parking lot on the afternoon of the killing. This way, those not well connected enough to secure tickets to view the actual killing can at least share part of the fun—and the satisfaction that always follows knowing you have just killed someone annoying for God.

Christian Hostess Tip:
When planning an execution tailgate party, remember that a softhearted governor can play havoc with your schedule, making a first-tier caterer difficult to pin down. Nevertheless, do your best to provide a convivial atmosphere with lovely heavy hors d'oeuvres in conspicuous counterpoint to the lie-berals who tend to bring little more than mawkish placards. Give me a lovely sandwich platter over a sandwich board any day!

who would betty stone?: a handy checklist so no sinner feels left out

SURVIVALTIP

1. Make a list of all the people the Old Testament encourages you to stone to death.

2. Remember, actions speak louder than words. Order stones.

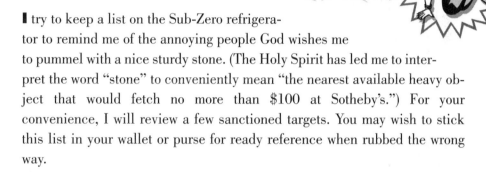

I try to keep a list on the Sub-Zero refrigerator to remind me of the annoying people God wishes me to pummel with a nice sturdy stone. (The Holy Spirit has led me to interpret the word "stone" to conveniently mean "the nearest available heavy object that would fetch no more than $100 at Sotheby's.") For your convenience, I will review a few sanctioned targets. You may wish to stick this list in your wallet or purse for ready reference when rubbed the wrong way.

People who dream and suggest you should follow another god
(Deuteronomy 13:5). I include Jehovah's Witnesses in this category—not because they technically follow another God, but because of the convenience of having them right there at your door.

Disobedient sons (Deuteronomy 21:18–21). As the parents of those odious Menendez sons discovered to their chagrin, this works only if the sons' act of disobedience is something other than defying the parent's request "please don't kill me!" A simple stoning certainly involves less messy clean-up than when the Lord commands you to eat your children (Deuteronomy 28:53). It also strikes me as a healthier pastime, involving more exercise and none of the saturated fats.

A bride who deceptively passes herself off as a virgin is to be taken by the men in the town and stoned to death (Deuteronomy 22:13–21). Mrs. Bowers' advice to those attending any American wedding: Forget the rice—take stones.

A child that curses his or her parent (Leviticus 20:9). If only that regrettable Mildred Pierce woman played by Joan Crawford had been an Orthodox Jew, her problems with her dreadful, sharp-tongued daughter Veda would have been solved rather expeditiously.

So close to Jesus,

*His shopping is
ruining my credit.*

A rapist—and the woman he raped for good measure! If an engaged virgin is raped in the city, both she and her assailant are to be stoned to death. God's logic? She could have screamed louder for help (Deuteronomy 22:24). Obviously the Lord has never had His purse snatched in Manhattan, where bellowing through a bullhorn would elicit only annoyance from strangers scurrying by to beat the flashing Walk light. If, however, the girl is not engaged, then the rapist must simply pay her father fifty shekels (roughly one Euro) and marry his victim. Personally, I can't imagine my own father pimping for so little money.

Adulterers (Deuteronomy 22:22). This rule has always worried me. Truly, do we have enough quarries?

WWBS?

What Would Betty Save?

her monthly quota of souls—and then herself the embarrassment of ascending to heaven with the poorly groomed!

SURVIVALTIP Try not to save people who are annoying. After all, what is the point of an eternity in Heaven if it only involves spending time with the people you avoided on Earth?

---

from the diary of america's best christian: *the price for saving the wrong people is an eternity of annoyance*

5:20 P.M., Atlanta, backseat of the ministry Bentley (the charcoal one)

I had a rather alarming dream last night. God was patiently explaining again to a gathering of the holy (Southern Baptists) in Heaven why it was that He created everything but is not responsible for anything. I initially thought His craftily worded explanation was clearly facetious and was prepared to indulge Him in the most convivial, lilting laugh (the type a friend uses to announce to a group that she is much closer to the person speaking because she is the only one to get an obtuse inside joke). Suddenly, I realized that God was absolutely serious in His self-absolution, so I allowed the beginning of my laugh to seamlessly segue into a delicate cough. No one, of course, noticed my cough because the air in Heaven, sitting as it does above the Northern Hemisphere, is about as clear as Mexican stemware.

Just as our Lord was getting to the part where He blames everything on His creation (us), as if to underscore His grievance, the Lord's dulcet, if too-loud, voice was undercut by the shrill braying of a pack of vulgar humans cresting a cloud. They were all wearing too-short shorts and T-shirts that attempted to converse with us. Completely oblivious to our jealous God's somewhat pathological need to be the constant center of attention, this group of unattractive people from Massapequa continued talking about how the pizza was better in New York. God, clearly annoyed by the rude intrusion, uncoiled the very finger that touched Adam's index finger and pointed it

So close to Jesus,
I'm number 3 on his speed dial.

at me. I, of course, raised an artfully drawn eyebrow, as I find it deplorable manners to point.

All of the Baptists gathered turned to look at me—on tenterhooks, no doubt, wondering what perfectly chosen phrase I would use to gently chide the Almighty. I was dressed exquisitely, but some, unfortunately, couldn't see me as their seat was not, of course, nearly as good as mine. Once everyone was looking in my direction, the Lord paused for effect (as if, considering the source, such dramatic touches are truly necessary) and bellowed with a sneer: "Betty saved them!" Everyone stared and tut-tutted. I, of course, was so embarrassed there was nothing left for me to do but make a dignified exit. I resourcefully feigned a forgotten meeting and rose slowly so as not allow the Lord the satisfaction of knowing that He had gotten to me. I then coolly walked, like Barbara Bain from *Mission Impossible* after she has just done something perilous, up the aisle to allow those in the back to see what Badgley Mischka has had the audacity to do this season. I then retreated to my lovely Milky Way–view mansion in the sky and had my seraphim help fetch a much-needed cocktail.

It was with this horrid dream in mind that I came to the conclusion that it might be a better use of my precious resources to make the American citizenry suitable for accommodations in Heaven before I impetuously ensure their arrival. It struck me as singularly imprudent to save anyone without regard to how infuriating they might be in Heaven.

SURVIVALTIP A good rule of thumb is that if someone happens to discover a way to get on your nerves in a mortal life, they will stumble upon countless other methods to infuriate you given a relentless eternity in which to work.

For _You_

Date _end_Times   **Urgent ☑**

While You Were Un-Saved

Mighty God

Of _heaven_

Phone   AREA CODE   NUMBER   EXTENSION

Fax

You were cursed ☐ to the 4th Generation

You were smote ☐ in a piqued moment

You were asked to ☐ sacrifice your first-born

Your mother was stoned to death ☐ by righteous Christian villagers

Message _Since you forgot to tell Jesus while you were alive that He was the most fabulous and kindest man to ever live, He will torture you forever_

Signed _Mrs. Betty Bowers_

WWBR?

Who Would Betty Rebuke?

letting lesser ideologues know their place —hell

betty bowers tells laura schlessinger: "i say this with much christian love, but you are simply too slutty to speak at my church, dear"

BETTY: Hello, Laura, are you there?

LAURA: Yes, I'm here. Your secretary had me on hold for almost twenty minutes.

BETTY: Well, at least your patience was rewarded, in contradistinction to those hapless souls who inexplicably call your little show.

LAURA: Now, wait just a minute, babe—

BETTY: Laura, please bottle your trademark "caustic impatience" shtick for the paying public. I have something rather important to discuss with you, and it will take far less time if you drop your anachronistic banter and some of your more threadbare antics, dear.

LAURA: Oh, not this again. Betty, I'm not going to convert back to Christianity, so save your breath, babe.

BETTY: Oh, heavens! I would *never* encourage you to do so. While I am somewhat obligated to, time permitting, save souls, it is my considered belief that having someone such as you in a high profile as a *non-Christian* can lead only to people flocking in droves to any faith other than your own—if only in flight from your peculiar brand of misanthropic piety.

LAURA: Oh, boy. Here we go. Get to your point.

If we wanted sluts in our church, we'd be Catholic.

63

BETTY: Gladly. You know how you are scheduled to speak at Landover Baptist this month?

LAURA: Yes, but I still haven't gotten my check for the thirty-thousand-dollar speaking fee.

BETTY: Yes, well, don't run out and add something to your collection of amusingly ostentatious jewelry in anticipation of its arrival, dear. You see, the Ladies of Landover had an emergency meeting last night, and we have prevailed upon Pastor to disinvite you. Naturally, I jumped at the chance to be the one to tell you this sad news.

LAURA: Wait a minute here—

BETTY: We just came to the regrettable—no matter how obvious—conclusion that you are just not "our type."

LAURA: Well, coming from you, I'll take that as a compliment. [*screech/laugh*]

BETTY: As you so rarely receive what could actually pass for a sincere compliment from someone with any self-esteem (which naturally excludes your callers), I shall overlook your obvious inability to recognize one, dear.

LAURA: Let me tell you what I think about that—

BETTY: Excuse me, dear, for interrupting. But you appear to be working under the notion that I happen to care about what you think. Whatever instinct led you to this erroneous conclusion should, under no circumstances, be trusted in the future. As I was saying, Mrs.—

LAURA: Doctor!

BETTY: Pardon?

LAURA: They call me "doctor."

BETTY: Well, they call you so many things, dear, it is rather hard to keep track. Fortunately for you I am too much of a lady to repeat all but a few of them. But since you are neither a medical doctor nor do you hold a doctorate degree in your chosen profession, your calling yourself "doctor" is nothing short of fraud and no more reflective of fact or binding on me than when Madonna refers to herself as "actress." In any event, what I was about to say is that the Landover Baptist Biblical Values Subcommittee discussed your visit to our church and determined that you don't live up to Landover Baptist's idea of traditional family values.

LAURA: Oh, boy! Babe, this is really making me want to scream—

BETTY: And with provocation, no less! How novel.

LAURA: Not consistent with traditional family values? Let me tell you something: I am known throughout this whole country—yes, little me—as being a voice in the wilderness for family values and—

BETTY: Your listeners' misapprehensions are not my concern, dear. But the type of person we at Landover put our reputation behind is. Quite frankly, it had not occurred to me that you were unsaved until one of my Sisters-in-Christ brought it to my attention.

LAURA: Jesus was born a Jew!

BETTY: And Michael Jackson was born black. People convert.

LAURA: Converted? But Jesus was always a Jew.

BETTY: Yes, but he wasn't a braying divorcée with a tongue that could lacerate a diamond cocktail ring. Surely you are not denying that you divorced.

LAURA: I feel that—

BETTY: Let's not talk about how you *feel;* let's talk about what you *are.* Let's stick to the facts. You were married before your current so-called marriage, weren't you?

LAURA: What do you mean "so-called"?

BETTY: Well, according to the Bible—the very same one you talk about but we *follow*—a woman can be married only once. *One.* Is that such a hard number to keep track of, dear? Just think of it as the number of seasons your little TV show *almost* made it through. Indeed, if a woman marries again, both she and her new "husband" are committing adultery (Matthew 5:32). So you are simply "shacking up with your honey." Such disgraceful conduct!

LAURA: There are *some* good reasons for divorce—

BETTY: Perhaps in your "me-me-me!" world of selfish morality, but not in the Bible. And we just can't have a known adulterer appear in our church. Especially one who keeps flaunting the fact that she has a bastard on national radio.

LAURA: A *bastard*?

BETTY: Well—*babe*—it stands to reason that if you're not married in the eyes of God, then any children are the spawn of an unholy union and therefore bastards. Such a harsh word, don't you think? I've never cared for it. Fortunately, I seldom have occasion to use it, as I don't move in the type of social circles where I run into women like you with any regularity. But I can just imagine how the word is like a fork in a filling to you, dear.

LAURA: I will not stand for you referring to my beloved bunchkin as a "bastard."

So close to Jesus, I know that the Holy Grail was dishwasher safe.

BETTY: And my Beloved Lord won't stand for you making him one, I assure you. Indeed, under Deuteronomy 23:2, he will be damned to the tenth generation. So isn't it time *you* took responsibility for *your* actions? It's lovely that you hawk T-shirts with the tautology "I Am My Kid's Mom," but wouldn't it have been better to have been able to wear one that says "I Am Married in the Eyes of God to My Kid's Father"? Just an idea, dear. And, honestly, those little pictures didn't help your cause.

LAURA: Oh, not them again! They were art pictures.

BETTY: Nudies! Taken by a man not your husband. Indeed, not even one of your many husbands. Hardly in keeping with the image you try so fecklessly to project.

LAURA: Those pictures were taken before I changed.

BETTY: Well, one look at those and anyone would change. Would that you had at least changed into a simple camisole. Such dreadful inattention to pubic grooming, dear! I mean, no one expects a mousse and curl, but a simple clip would not have been remiss.

LAURA: The point I am making is that I am not a hypocrite.

BETTY: I didn't say those pictures make you a hypocrite, dear. A *slut,* perhaps. But now that you mention it, you are a hypocrite for the impatient way you treat the mistakes of your foolish callers. Clearly, you committed worse errors of judgment than most of them in your, uh, *distant* youth. So, your acting as if your callers are complete idiots in their more immediate youth is not only rude, it is rather hypocritical of you, dear. Well, I must say, hardly a startling discovery there! In any event, consider yourself rebuked and uninvited.

LAURA: Now wait just one minute! It's time someone told you—

BETTY: Dear, I am trying to care about what you think. Truly, I am. But, so far, nothing is working. And as you seem so utterly unable to one-up me, might I suggest that you instead settle for one up yours? Good day. [*Dial tone*]

...Saved Souls UP...Demons DOWN 13...Whore of Babylon DOWN 69 (in heavy trading)...Holy Trinity UP 7 (in a 3-for-1 split)...God's Wrath DOWN 7/8...God's Mercy UP 3/8...Landover Baptist Preferred UP 18...Vatican, Inc. DOWN 5/8...Mrs. Betty Bowers Ministries UP 387 (trading halted to give other spiritual stocks a chance for redemption)...Satan DOWN...Praise the Lord!

WWBW?

What Would Betty Watch?

hollywood trash so you don't have to—and then her perfect size 4 waist!

Betty's HOLYWOOD

betty's list of movies with acceptable christian messages

The Wizard of Oz. This film beautifully instills too-often-neglected Christian values. Viz., when you are having more fun than you have ever had in your otherwise dreary life, it is time to feel guilty and cry. You must then, of course, flee your colorful new world where you actually have friends who don't bark. To do this, endanger everyone's life so that you might return to a relentlessly drab world with a humorless self-proclaimed "Christian woman" who lives in a rickety shack in the middle of a patch of dust. Jesus suffered—why shouldn't you?

The Way We Were. A handsome Christian boy should never marry an unsaved Communist—regardless of the number of hours she devotes to how well she is lit.

All About Eve. If only the original Eve had combined her inclination to deceive with this Eve's polished obsequiousness when dealing with the easily flattered, we might all have perfectly landscaped homes in Metropolitan Eden today.

The Godfather. Since all Catholics are going to Hell anyway, they apparently embrace their fate as a license to dress without taste and kill without provocation. The theme of this film is similar to that in *West Side Story:* Become involved with a Catholic, wind up dead.

Rear Window. People can be alarmingly surreptitious when sinning in the so-called "privacy" of their homes. And how are you ever to rebuke sinners for things you don't make an effort to witness? This film is a clarion call to all True Christians™ to show concern for the welfare of their neighbors through vigilant and constant surveillance. The film also underscores the power of a smart tailored skirt when trying to enthrall the latently homosexual.

The Grapes of Wrath. A good rule of thumb when fleeing unpleasantness is if you can fit all your earthly belongings in one car, don't expect things to be much more comfortable when you arrive at wherever it is you are going.

A Clockwork Orange. In case the lesson of this movie was not clear, we have Michael Jackson to remind us: The police should keep a constant eye on men who wear mascara.

Amadeus. The writing of a charming symphony may please a theater audience, but the memory of a crude flatulence joke lasts a lifetime. The message is clear: No matter how talented he is at his chosen craft, a coarse artist without appropriate table manners deserves to be tossed into an unmarked grave.

Forrest Gump. Stupidity never trumps serendipity or an overbearing mother. Just ask George W. Bush.

So close to Jesus,
I probably think this Psalm
is about me.

betty's list of forbidden movies with deplorable messages

Casablanca. Humphrey Bogart and Ingrid Bergman consoled themselves by saying that they would "always have Paris." I think they unnecessarily sold their shared travelogue rather short. Adulterers will, after all, always have Hell, too.

It's a Wonderful Life. This pernicious confection teaches the outrageous lie that people who attempt suicide will exchange banter with angels—instead of bodily fluids with demons.

The Graduate. Perhaps a sexually frustrated, married harlot like Mrs. Robinson should take her own husband's advice—look into plastics.

Some Like It Hot. And it is just as well! Men who enjoy frolicking in chiffon drop-waist shifts and perilous pumps had better pack sleeveless, as it doesn't get any hotter than Hell.

Snow White and the Seven Dwarfs. Dorothy Gale of *The Wizard of Oz* showed questionable social instincts relying upon immediately killing someone to make a favorable first impression on her new neighbors. Nevertheless, in contradistinction to the promiscuous harlot Miss White, when Miss Gale was first introduced to a pack of short men offering something to lick at least her first impulse wasn't to move in with them!

The African Queen. As a True Christian™ I have never seen this movie, but does the world really need a cinematic biography of Johnny Mathis?

2001: A Space Odyssey. This propaganda for secular science would have us believe we started as poorly groomed apes that brandished bones as our first step to building machines that would one day destroy us. Alas, this film's projection of the future has proved to be as inaccurate as its reflection on the past. Our present-day computers are more likely to annoy us with unwanted e-mail hawking a pyramid scheme than to outsmart us with patronizing conversation.

Butch Cassidy and the Sundance Kid. The message of this film is greatly troubling. Being an avid reader of the Old Testament, I don't bat an eye at gratuitous killing, but I am deeply suspicious of two beautiful blond men who flee the company of a naked woman to run off together.

The Sound of Music. Judging from this Austrian brood, but for a timely death, "Sixteen Going on Seventeen" would probably have been an accurate count of their obviously Catholic mother's pregnancies. As for Maria, while I admire any woman who is resourceful enough to acquire a Baroque mansion (on a lovely lake, no less!) for a song, I cannot approve of nuns marrying men, no matter how handsome or adept with their whistles. After all, Catholic nuns are supposed to be already married to Jesus, and while Jesus is at times alarmingly open-minded, He is not a Mormon.

Giant. Rock Hudson and James Dean fight over Elizabeth Taylor. Was it really necessary to make a movie this long to show how homosexuals vie for Miss Taylor's attention?

roman holler/slay: christian persecution is back in style in hollywood! betty reviews the film *gladiator*

Sitting in my stadium seat listening to an uncouth secular audience raucously cheering *Gladiator*, I felt like a rabbi at the Nuremberg rallies. But instead of the crowd whooping it up for an unattractive little man who, all for the want of a fistful of Prozac, killed off half of Europe, the audience at *Gladiator* was screaming for Christian blood. My blood.

Using men with bulging biceps, bulging chests, and, well, things that were bulging that no Christian woman should ever have thrust in her face, *Gladiator* will do more for homoerotic Christian mayhem than anything since Caligula first sashayed into the Colosseum. *Gladiator*, a film that manages to be crafty without craft, is littered with offensive antifamily propaganda and a level of vulgarity not commonly seen outside of Nevada.

Russell Crowe stars as General Maximus, a downwardly mobile Roman who is forced into the most base of all professions—show business. He entertains at amphitheaters throughout suburban Rome by decapitating Christians with an unrefined swagger too gruff to remind one of any genuine heterosexual males. Indeed, his technique clearly draws on the exaggeratedly robust manliness that can be found only in women's professional basketball.

Maximus is certainly no Christian. Indeed, watching him cart around a leather pouch with a couple of graven images to worship, I initially assumed that he was a Catholic. However, in a galling act of one-upmanship, instead of worshiping simply a son who has been crucified, Maximus spends the movie worshiping both a son *and a mother* who have been crucified. Are we supposed to be happy that this pagan looks forward to an afterlife in a place he calls "Elysium" instead of "Heaven"? It is almost as if the screenwriter were implying that Christianity is just some wholly derivative religion!

What will every True Christian™ despise about this movie? Let's start with the vulgar name attached to the project. It doesn't take a cryptographer to unlock the salacious wordplay of the title to this trashy homage to amorality. Of the seven women from Bringing Integrity To Christian Homemakers who attended the screening with me, only one did not immediately pick up on the shockingly lewd subliminal message glaring down on us in twelve-foot letters. As my dear Sister-in-Christ, the eighty-one-year-old Mrs. Helen Floribunda pointed out: "It really takes a sick, sick, secular mind to give a movie a title like

Christian Hostess Tip: Quite the flamboyant host, God asked prophets to throw a party to eat the flesh of mighty men and get drunk on the blood of princes (Ezekiel 39:18). However, I would caution any modern hostess to consult with her guests about any doctor-ordered dietary restrictions before going to the expense and trouble of replicating the Lord's fare.

that just to get a puerile giggle out of good, wholesome Christians going around town saying 'Glad He Ate Her.'"

Let's talk about the sick way that the men dress for a minute. Most eschew the modesty of an ankle-length belted senatorial toga for a more racy gladiator miniskirt with leather/armor kick pleats. It is a look perversely Jean Paul Gaultier in its decadent homoeroticism and sassy mix of fabrics. Of course, there is a sick purpose behind the Carnaby Street altitude of the men's skirts, which are far too short for even the most brazen female—such as, say, a Catholic schoolgirl. The skirts provide ample opportunity for the voyeuristic Steadicam operators brazenly to play peek-a-boo with half of the cast's crotches. I counted eighty-six salacious "genital bulge" shots—seven of which were in a decidedly turgid state. In fact, there may well have been more, but I was so utterly overwhelmed by how the character Maximus lived up to his name, I simply lost count. Thank the Lord I was proactive enough to pack a moist towelette in my Prada clutch.

Yes, the film is prurient. But what can we expect from an amoral smut mill like Hollywood? With *Gladiator*, Hollywood has shed any pretense that it has not been co-opted as the Joseph Goebbels of the Homosexual Agenda. The movie is confected of two things notoriously homosexual: (a) sweaty, muscular men impaling each other within moments of meeting; and (b) an exquisite placement of period furniture.

By selling tickets at the Colosseum, the Romans discovered that Christian persecution is a huge moneymaking opportunity. This ancient economics lesson has not been lost on modern businesses. Traditional Values Coalition, Focus on the Family and the Christian Coalition have all co-opted with alacrity the Roman flare for turning even faux persecution into real dollars.

But let's not allow all those plentiful "love offerings" to cause us to let our guard down. Surely we are only a year away from devoted, yet wiry, Christians being pummeled on the mat at World Wide Wrestling in "Baptist Slapdowns"—to the delight of atheist hillbillies with access to cable. Mark my words: When Ticketmaster begins selling seats throughout this once-great land to "Christians vs. Visiting Lions," you will look back and know that this "sport" was all started by that seemingly harmless homosexual cult movie *Gladiator*.

Mrs. Bowers gives it a thumbs down.

betty's exclusive interview: rapper eminem is born again!

Anyone watching MTV will tell you that Marshall Mathers, also known as Eminem, Slim Shady, and "Defendant," has broken out like psoriasis. After listening to his angry tirades filled with juvenile angst and contrived mayhem, I expected a rough man to saunter into my suite at the Four Seasons for our interview. I was not prepared for the fey, timid little boy who has, no doubt, grown up under a barrage of taunts and insults (those directed at his "look" would certainly fall comfortably under the expanding heading of "constructive criticism"). It is with guarded jubilation that I discovered that this trailer tenor has become a born-again Christian. I also have an exclusive preview of Eminem's new CD, which is inspired entirely by Bible verses. Being based on our Lord's Old Testament, of course, it will present no discernible departure from his previous misogynistic and bloodthirsty rants.

BETTY: So tell us: Whom did Christina Aguilera pleasure first?

EMINEM: Carson, then Fred.

BETTY: Well, one look at that harlot, my only surprise is that she waited to do them one at a time. Now, to you: I didn't realize you were an albino.

EMINEM: I ain't no fucking albino! You want to dwell on my race, but you could *never* say that my shit is wack because you know my shit is tight.

BETTY: Scatological speculation aside, tell us, are you now a born-again Christian?

EMINEM: Yeah, I am down with the Bible.

BETTY: How did this miraculous change occur, dear?

EMINEM: Well–*dear*–see? Everywhere I turn, people are trying to dog me about not being "politically correct" and shit. You know? People saying, "You ain't supposed to say 'faggot,'" and "You ain't supposed to talk bout beating up bitches." And Dr. Dre say–

Biblical Shopping Tip: Picking the perfect gift has never been easy— even when just quickly shopping for *other* people. Just look at the three so-called Wise Men. One was crass enough to give gold—the biblical equivalent of a gift certificate. The other two showed up with frankincense and myrrh, proving once again that when men have no idea what you want, they give you fragrance. At least baby Jesus didn't have to feign delight unwrapping lingerie two sizes too small in odious shades of red.

BETTY: What type of doctor is the no-doubt-charming Dr. Dre anyway? Medical? Ph.D.?

EMINEM: Dre ain't a doctor. He just calls himself that to sound important.

BETTY: Oh, sort of like Dr. Laura.

EMINEM: She is one hard bitch.

BETTY: Perhaps you two could do a duet. You seem to hate all the same people.

EMINEM: Yeah, but I hate her, too! [*Laughs*]

BETTY: Well, that hardly sets you apart, dear.

EMINEM: Yeah, but she wouldn't be down with it since she isn't going to cooperate with my slams on her.

BETTY: No, self-hatred would require far too much introspection for her. Let's talk about something more pleasant. So, I take it from your charming deportment today that you didn't become born again to renounce coarse, secular vulgarity.

EMINEM: No, bitch. I didn't fucking get fucking born again to do that!

BETTY: This is clearly a metamorphosis in its very earliest of stages. I assume, at a minimum, that you will no longer sing about such uncivil inclinations as killing.

EMINEM: Killing? Everyone is riding me about violence. Look, *Saving Private Ryan* was probably the illest, sickest movie I've ever watched, and I didn't see anybody criticizing that one for violence.

BETTY: That killing was done for the Lord, dear. Indeed, the bullets our boys fired were from God in Heaven. The German bullets were coming, of course, straight from Satan. And the French . . . well, there were no French bullets, were there? But I'm always grateful the French are cowards every time I wander among the unblemished buildings of Paris. *Vive la indifférence!* Anyway, everyone America kills either has crude morals or crude oil. And all American war efforts are for the glory of God and General Dynamics.

EMINEM: Yeah, like carpet-bombing civilians in Dresden just 'cause we were pissed off at the end of World War Two? How is that different than a punk fucked over and pissed just taking a semi to some fucking fools at a shopping mall?

BETTY: Because those deaths are not paid for by tax dollars, dear. Anyway, let's get back to your purported religious conversion. What led you to Jesus? My website?

EMINEM: No. (Laughs) It was Reverend Louis Sheldon from Traditional Values Coalition.

BETTY: Oh, I adore Louis. After reading his newsletters, it is clear that he seldom allows a moment to pass without thinking about men licking each other. He is so utterly selfless.

EMINEM: Well, whatever, lady. Sheldon called me on the cell and told me that if I became a Bible worshiper, it would help me out a lot with the press. See?

BETTY: By accepting Jesus Christ as your Personal Savior?

EMINEM: No. Follow me, bitch. You see, Traditional Values Coalition pays for all these focus groups and they know just what to say to the press. By being able to say that I was just stating my "Christian religious beliefs" instead of just personal stuff, they told me I could say all kinds of shit and no one could touch me about it. Not even *Newsweek*. And what Sheldon said made sense. And so I read the Bible for the first time and I was down with it. God represents. I mean, God hates all the same people I do. He's cool! So now, when I sing about hating fags and women, I can say, "Hey man, I'm just expressing my religious views here, man!" And if anyone dares to question me, I just say: "You're persecuting me for religious beliefs!" And how can they argue with that? God in the Old Testament said, "Stone the fags! Kill the bitches!" See? I give props to Sheldon. He knows how to work it. So now, those faggots at *Time* and *Rolling Stone* can't touch me 'cause on my next CD everything is going to be totally tied into the Bible. And you wouldn't believe the fucking shit God has going down! I mean, here is an example of sample:

> Take a good look, at the Good Book, when you hit my shit with the tag "he's misogynistic!"
> It's inherent, see? From inerrant me! That apparently, if He sees a bitch or fag, God goes ballistic.
> You see, when the Lord is mad, shit, then you know Yahweh has had it!
> If you've been acting shitty, God says: "Have no pity!
> Slay the punks, slay the bitches!"
> Lord, what about their brats? "Slay those rats; leave 'em bleeding in the ditches!" [Ezekiel 9: 4–6]
> Destroy their hood—kill 'em good [I Samuel 15:2–3]. Yo, go to every city purging

75

Set your sights on the whites of their eyes, but keep a prize—all them
pretty virgins! [Numbers 31:17–18]

And all the pansy press is, in their dresses, saying, "Slim, why you say-
ing faggots should die?"

And I just raise my Bible high: "The Lord said you got to go, so, homo,
that's fucking why!" [laughs] [Leviticus 20:13]

And all you ragheads with the wrong god, get my drift, here's a gift: six
feet of your own sod! [Exodus 22:20]

Now, I am turning to Saint Paul. He said it all, in his letters to Timothy.
See?

All you hos in the place, shut your face and take commands from me!
[1 Timothy 2:11–12]

BETTY: See what I am doing? I am writing you a check for fifty thousand dollars—out of my tax-free ministry Emergency Relief Fund—as it is truly an emergency to get you to stop whatever it is you are doing at once, dear. While, I am sure, it is infinitely more egalitarian not to restrict the making of music to those who actually know anything about it, my Krups coffee grinder offers a more dulcet facsimile of melody—and I can always unplug that.

from the diary of america's best christian: *taking time to find the sins more careless christians overlook*

3:03 P.M., Barnes & Noble, Atlanta

I did my weekly stop by local bookstores to check for child pornography masquerading as "art" books. I was disappointed to find none . . . this time. While I was browsing for signs of immorality (and surreptitiously transcribing recipes from Gunter Seeger's fabulous new cookbook onto index cards), I came across a few Lewis Carroll books. It was like Botox to both sides of my smile. His books seemed to be resting on the wooden shelf simply to taunt me. Just last year, I had spearheaded an unsuccessful campaign to remove *Alice in Wonderland* from the shelves of public school libraries in one of Atlanta's suburban counties. Clearly, this subversive story encourages Christian children to question what they are told, placing Christian parents in the untenable position of having to explain to youngsters why the God who loves them will probably torture them in Hell. The school board, under the red-hot hoof of Lucifer, denied my request to ban the book. Indeed, I noted one barely subdued snigger during voting from someone I had pegged as clearly unsaved. Not daunted when doing the Lord's work, I immediately turned my attention to Carroll's other writings to see if any of them would be easier targets. I knew "Jabberwocky" *should* be banned, because anything that unintelligible must be as subversive as James Joyce. But since I could never quite articulate a specific reason for my instinctive disapproval, I reluctantly let the matter drop, mindful of that odious snigger. But I was, of course, having the last laugh. Since September, I have relocated countless volumes of Lewis Carroll in bookstores throughout Atlanta to places I was certain no one would ever venture. This time, I placed them right between two copies of an autobiography by Victoria Principal.

What Would Betty Say?

"you are going straight to hell"—and then an imprecatory prayer for your swift departure

interview with diane sawyer

DIANE: Mrs. Bowers, welcome. You look really lovely—as always.

BETTY: Thank you, dear. You know, Barbara Walters and I were just speculating over lunch that you would look absolutely stunning in the right clothes— [*Off-the-record discussion ensues.*] Anyway, what I meant was that we must all bring Glory to our Lord in our own particular way. And if He chooses to use my perfect size-4 frame and regal carriage to delight His followers with the flawless nuance of top Italian designers, then who am I, as His humble servant, to eschew such a specific calling? Indeed, I find that I can seldom say no to my Lord.

DIANE: Wait a minute. Seldom?

BETTY: Well, sometimes He goes a little beyond the bounds of reason, to say nothing of etiquette, in His requests. I mean, we are talking about someone who thinks nothing of asking people to kill their children. Not that He's a hypocrite—He's certainly willing to lead by example. Just ask Jesus. But still. Sometimes, He will ask something that causes me to raise a perfectly penciled eyebrow.

DIANE: You mean you would defy your Lord?

BETTY: Oh, never. That would be a sin. I just don't act upon the request right away. That shrewd recalcitrance is probably the only reason I still have two children. And if I give it enough time, the Lord usually forgets about it, and it never comes up again. I certainly never bring it up.

DIANE: Mrs. Bowers, you don't mean to imply that the Almighty is forgetful, do you?

BETTY: Well, I don't know why you have that look of shock on your face, dear. Our Lord is notoriously absentminded. I mean—true story—He created Adam and Eve knowing they would disobey. But once they were alive, and Eve was enjoying the one time in our planet's history when a husband didn't have anyone to cheat with, God forgot all about how scurrilous humans were going to be. Why do you think He got so angry when they sinned? They thought He was just feigning surprise—you know, into the drama of the whole thing—but He had actually totally forgotten. Completely!

DIANE: Do Southern Baptists believe in forgiveness?

BETTY: Yes, absolutely. But just because one forgives does not mean that one forgets. I may forgive one of my shiftless domestic help for breaking a lovely piece of Sèvres porcelain. But that doesn't mean I'm going to forget about it when I dock her pay at the end of the month. Similarly with God. He may forgive you your trespasses (or, more often than not with His memory, simply let them slip His mind), but that doesn't mean they won't pop into His head come Judgment Day.

DIANE: Well, it appears that God is more forgiving than you are, Mrs. Bowers.

BETTY: Well, perhaps some leniency is called for when one is responding with eternal torture, rather than simply a frosty glare across a crowded party, dear. But even so, the Lord did say that there is one unforgivable sin.

DIANE: What is the one thing that is so horrible that even God can't forgive you for it?

BETTY: Making a snide remark about the Holy Ghost. [Matthew 12:31]

DIANE: Just the Ghost? What if I blaspheme God?

BETTY: You can be forgiven for that, dear.

DIANE: What about if I blaspheme Jesus—the focal point of Christianity?

BETTY: Diane, don't make me go through a tiresome litany of would-be obvious, but nevertheless incorrect, choices, dear. The rule is quite simple. You can make a lifetime hobby of blaspheming anyone you wish—even God—and you will be forgiven. But just one slip of the tongue about the Holy Spirit, and you are on a one-way ride to Hell.

DIANE: That doesn't make any sense.

BETTY: I know it seems unfair that someone can, say, murder a child and ask for forgiveness and it will be given—but if they simply murmur something untoward about the Holy Spirit, all hope is lost. But I don't make the rules, dear. God does. And apparently the Holy Spirit is a rather fragile little thing that can't bear criticism. Let's face it, Diane, we've all known people like that. [*Off-the-record conversation ensues.*]

DIANE: Mrs. Bowers—may I call you Betty?

BETTY: No. Only my Savior calls me Betty. And that was only after many years and no small reluctance on my part. I think familiarity is tacky and shows a deplorable lack of breeding. Of course, Jesus was born in a stable, but still, He's had long enough to learn better, and I can't allow that type of faux intimacy. Oh, dear, look at the time. I really must go.

DIANE: But I have just one more question. It'll take only a minute.

BETTY: Well, that would be one more minute than I agreed to, dear.

DIANE: I thought you would stay at least thirty minutes.

BETTY: Oh, dear. How delicious! I never do a half hour for this kind of money. Besides, the Bowers Ministry Bentley is waiting to take me to the Bowers Ministry plane. I'm already late.

DIANE: Where are you going?

BETTY: Saudi Arabia. I don't care for Arabs—naturally—but they have oodles of money. They may front some Swiss cash for a hostile takeover of the Trinity Broadcasting Network. All *entre nous*, of course, dear. It appears that a deep-seated abhorrence of that tacky Jezebel Jan Crouch is utterly cross-cultural, which is making lining up backing a snap from Geneva to Abu Dhabi. Oh, please be a dear and call my assistant, Miss Anne Thrope. Tell her to go out to the Gulfstream and inspect the food. It's a long flight, and last time the pineapple was decidedly Mexican. Dreadful. I almost lost a tooth.

So close to Jesus,

He designates me on forms that require someone to contact in case of emergency (as His Father has forsaken him).

epistle of profound and compassionate christian advice:
school prayer and other ways of getting back at jews for killing jesus

So-called near-death experiences are a constant source of irritation to an already irascible Lord. All too often, He goes to all the trouble of hauling out the bright lights and doing the whole "welcome to Heaven" production—only to find that human doctors have outsmarted him and brought the patient back to life.

Dear Betty:

Recently, my daughter, who wears a one-and-a-half-inch-long crucifix around her throat, completed the Christian conversion of her car with a palm leaf cross on the dashboard, a Jesus ornament hanging from the rearview mirror, a Christian fish decal stuck on her back window, and a "Jesus Paid the Price—but Visa Declined the Charge" bumper sticker. I was raised to believe that your religious faith is something personal between you and God. I find my daughter's ostentatious displays sort of tacky, but I don't know how to bring up the topic without her trying loudly to call demons out of me in a public restaurant.

Yours in faith.

Bothered in Beaufort, S.C.

FROM THE LOUIS QUINZE DESK OF

Betty Bowers

AMERICA'S BEST CHRISTIAN

Dear Hellbound Sinner:

We live in a country founded on the principles that (a) possession is pointless without acknowledgment and, preferably envy, and (b) quiet people are usually hiding something. Therefore, in American Christianity, having a "personal" savior is not like having a "personal" thought or a "personal" problem. Instead, it is more akin to having a "personal" billboard. Yes, it is yours, but there isn't much point in acquiring it unless everyone who passes notices.

You could, I suppose, pray silently, but isn't it far more engaging—to say nothing of energetic—to get up in front of the entire congregation and do an "altar call" sprint or flop about like a dockside marlin in the aisle "slain in the Spirit"? Why, after all, should our faith be all about the worshiped, with little attention given to those who actually perform the onerous legwork of worshiping?

As a Fundamentalist Christian, I must, of course, make some passing reference to what the eponym of our faith has said when He appears to contradict my wishes. Yes, Jesus did make some noise about not wanting us to pray in public. In fact, He specifically said that people who pray in public are just doing it to show off and would pray in a closet if they really meant it (Matthew 6:5–6).

Fortunately for us, Jesus' admonitions must often be inverted by the rather nimble Holy Spirit to be understood in a way that comports with American Christianity. You see, Jesus lived before the Advertising Age, when America experimented with selling plastic things and ideas to the public. That worked for a while, but everyone eventually became too jaded to believe anything inconvenient. Now, in the Post-Advertising Age, we are reveling in an era when members of the pub-

lic devote all of their time to advertising the one thing that means the most to them—themselves! That is why everyone goes on television to reveal personal information that Mrs. Bowers wouldn't admit in a darkened chalk wine cellar fifty feet below Reims, France, to an empty bottle of Pommery.

If you look closely at recent social trends, it appears that the one thing we Real Americans now enjoy advertising the most is just how much more Christian our children are than the children of Jews at local public schools. That is why we get so terribly annoyed when hellbound liberals pull the plug on the 1,000-watt pregame amplification system. The secular Supreme Court has trampled American Christians' constitutional right to something we all hold dear—deafeningly loud prayer.

Once, the flagpole was a place to gather around to say, "Isn't it nice we are all Americans?" Nowadays, it provides a focal point to ask, "Isn't it suspicious that you aren't a Christian?" It is within the context of our national crusade to loudly brandish matters of so-called "personal" faith that I find your daughter's rather anemic attempts to inform others of her religious beliefs deplorably timid. Such halfhearted efforts to advertise her faith, as if she were reluctantly selling Amway, are displeasing to the more market-driven Jesus of today. I suggest having her talk to the people who made the Oscar Meyer hot-dog car about converting her vehicle into a fiberglass Golgotha-bound savior on wheels. Please caution her, however, that in most states she will be required by law to attach a bright red flag to the bottom of the cross's vertical beam.

So close to Jesus, the Jews don't believe in me either,

Betty Bowers

HWBR?

How Would Betty React?

from the diary of america's best christian: *what to do when your personal savior stops by without calling first*

6:35 A.M., Bowers' co-op, Manhattan

Just as I was passing through the main hallway, Jesus appeared to me in the Louis Seize mirror near the staircase. Since I was in a bit of a rush, I pretended not to notice Him. I adore Him more than my suite at the Crillon, but since deities are forever, they have no concept of time, which makes them virtually indistinguishable from Spaniards. For example, He *says* He whipped up the universe in the same amount of time it takes one-note comedians to throw a *Saturday Night Live* show together. I'm uncertain whether such remarks spring from the Lord's machismo boasting or simply because, bless Him, He's been around so long He can't tell the difference between an epoch and a hiccup. In any event, when the Lord tells you "Let's get together tomorrow," there is no need to cancel your luncheon plans for the following day. Trust me; I've learned the hard way. Obviously the Apostle Paul was not quite so savvy, as he appears to have taken Jesus' promise to return "soon" quite seriously. Two thousand years (and counting) is "soon" to Jesus, which is why I never make reservations with Him at a restaurant that won't seat you until your entire party has arrived.

I dropped the faxes of the Nikkei averages I was holding in disgust on the Jean-Henri Ricener commode under the Beauvais and made my way to the elevator. My considered fear of what was going to happen when the New York markets opened caused me to forget completely that my Personal Savior was in the room. Not the type of oversight I am particularly proud of, as I do consider myself

85

to be an exemplary hostess. I indulged myself in a quick look in the lovely Bonzanigo mirror that I had outbid Philippe Starck for at Sotheby's (by having him called out to the lobby by some unsaved person who looked as if he'd do anything for a crisp $100 bill). I wanted to see if I looked as youthful as I had in the mirrors I had checked upstairs. There appeared to be a unanimous consensus from all my furniture at this point, so I knew it was time to go. But the Italian mirror caught the reflection of Jesus in the French mirror across the hall, resulting in a gently curving greenish arc of hundreds of beveled saviors at quarter-inch intervals. He was splayed out like a pack of Jacks looking over my shoulder in stern reproach. It was rather disconcerting.

I had a brief moment of indecision. I wanted to say hello to Him, but Jesus knows that I have no patience for people who stop by without calling first. To acknowledge them only encourages them. And this is bad enough with people who need keys. And I find that when speaking with deities, it is always about them. So I quite artfully conjured a state of mind utterly foreign to me. Obliviousness.

Slipping on my black Armani raincoat, I picked up my Bible. Ignoring Jesus' face, I feigned interest in His word, by intently flipping through I Samuel as I glided into the waiting elevator. As I turned, I allowed the perfectly weighted hem of my coat to insouciantly swirl while I pretended to notice Jesus for the first time. I couldn't tell from His expression whether or not He was buying it because He seemed to be admiring the line of my coat. With one hand, I appeared to reach to stop the doors from closing, with the other I surreptitiously pressed the Close button and was on my way to a lovely breakfast.

Christian Hostess Tip: Have your help fill your home with fresh flowers from the garden in case your Personal Savior drops in uninvited. Remember that carnations are never welcome outside of a public school prom and the Lord has been overheard to remark that star lilies smell like "old French whores." From the tone of His voice, I was unable to discern if this last comment was spoken out of chagrin or fond remembrance, but a prudent hostess will play it safe and avoid them. Don't, under any circumstances, resort to roses. When doing a centerpiece for Jesus, thorns are an outrageously thoughtless touch.

how would betty react?

86

Where Would Betty Go?

to extremes to be america's most selfless christian—and then to her suite at the villa d'este on lake como for a month!

CHARITY: surprising those who think they have everything with charming gifts of the holy spirit

WELCOME SENORA BOWERS

After two somewhat successful, yet thankless, years of helping people without sufficient breeding to convey gratitude with any regularity or panache, I decided to redirect Christians Having A Righteously Itemized Tax Year's vast resources and lovely stationery. CHARITY will now turn its attention to helping the fabulously wealthy—for truly, as the Lord reminds us, CHARITY should begin at home. For the past eight months, I have been marshaling an admittedly strident campaign to remind people that their salvation depends on owning and, to a lesser extent, reading a quality Bible. With an almost seven-figure budget, I have quite selflessly traveled the world bringing the Lord's Good News, alternating my stays between lovely inns known only to the travel cognoscenti and Leading Hotels of the World and Relais & Chateaux properties. I have traveled tirelessly so that no exclusive resort feels shunned by God's love. These visits provide me with perfect opportunities to provide the dining room help at each five-star hotel with an unblemished view of what a Christian with taste actually looks like (the Lord told us to not hide our light) and a gentle reminder that when it comes to tips from Baptists, waiters' rewards will not be in *this* life.

As the centerpiece of this godly mission, I have taken a moment away from lovely meals at the villas of local Christian patriarchs and private tours of pagan (Catholic) cathedrals to exorcise from my lovely hotel suite any deplorably bound and heretically translated Gideons' Bibles (also known as Not-So-Good Books). After flinging the offending book to the pavement and/or courtyard below, it is replaced with a charming King James Version sporting a supple Italian leather cover more worthy of the Lord and the reproduction drawer that holds it. My itinerant multimillion-dollar CHARITY hotel ministry has brought joy to literally *tens* of people. And lovely, plush, crested bathrobes to most of my closest friends.

So close to Jesus,
I know His AOL password.

SURVIVALTIP Make sure you have a Bible that boasts a translation God approves of, as no one likes to see their literary efforts mangled or made pedestrian by the all too appropriately titled "plain English." I fully realize that the sodomite King James was not our sort, but homosexuals, though damned, are traditionally very good with words. (You see, the Lord has given homosexuals a heightened sense of aesthetics only so that Hell's garish look will be even more punishment to them.) Therefore, I tip my beguiling hat to King James—as he screams in agony under a sharp pitchfork in Hell—and thank him for such a lovely translation.

epistle of profound and compassionate christian advice: *why was jesus born in a place without air-conditioning?*

Dear Mrs. Bowers:

You act as if the only people who will end up in Heaven will be Americans. If this were true, why did God send Jesus to our part of the world?

Miffed in Jerusalem

FROM THE LOUIS QUINZE DESK OF

Betty Bowers

AMERICA'S BEST CHRISTIAN

Dear Hellbound Sinner:

Our Lord Jesus Christ lived in your arid neck of the woods only because the whole purpose of His visit was to suffer for our sins, dear. Short of actually being crucified, a summer in the dusty Middle East without air-conditioning is about as uncomfortable as a god-made man can get. Add to that your deplorable indigenous cuisine, and Jesus' gesture veers from the selfless to the masochistic.

Had He wished to come in glory and live in the glamorous style of the Hereafter, He would have, of course, waited 2,000 years and visited me in my lovely Italianate manse nestled in the expensively landscaped glades of Atlanta. I'm sure he would have found my food sublime, my staff unobtrusive, and my reluctance to pester for miracles refreshing. Further, I would have ensured that His last supper would have been more memorable than three courses in a public restaurant. (No wonder our Lord rebuked Mary—a woman too lazy to prepare her son a home-cooked meal on His last night on Earth.) After becoming accustomed to such lovely hospitality, voluntarily climbing on a cross to be killed truly would have been an amazing sacrifice.

So close to Jesus, we are thinking of—finally—taking separate vacations this year,

Betty Bowers

Biblical Shopping Tip: "The Lord saith, Provide purses for yourselves that will not wear out" (Luke 12:33). The Lord clearly goes for quality, not cheap Chinese knockoffs, girls!

HWBM?

How Would Betty Mother?

don't brag about your conception if your christian home is not also immaculate!

sometimes a "distant father" is not such a bad thing

Out-of-wedlock teenage pregnancy? A distant, angry father nowhere in sight? Yes, Mary and God are not what I would hold up as an example of the ideal Christian parents. In fact, Mary and God showed such a lackadaisical approach to child rearing, I am honestly surprised that Jesus turned out so wonderfully! After all, this is a father who had his son conceived by proxy (a bird through the ear of a woman he had never even taken on one date, much less married) and raised by another man. Then, the father ignored his son, showing up thirty years later to say, "Oh, by the way, I only had you to kill you." Talk about an absentee, abusive parent!

SURVIVALTIP When faced with a less-than-perfect child, it is wise to stone him before he is strong enough to respond in kind—just in case your aim also proves to be less than perfect.

Nevertheless, it is hard to argue with the happy results. Jesus was rather exemplary in everything but his inexplicable penchant for wearing burlap and Birkenstocks. Indeed, had the cantankerous, vain, and wrathful God we know from the Old Testament played a greater role in raising Jesus, Jesus would probably never have had said all those loving, humble, and pacifistic things for which He is now most famous. So, perhaps we should be grateful that God is so neglectful that He must resort to foster care for His only child.

In any event, it would hardly seem fair to fault Mary for being less than an ideal mother. Just look at what she had to consult for guidance in child rearing—the Old Testament.

raising cain: earth's first halfhearted attempt at parenting

The first lesson we learn in the Bible: Women can't be trusted. The second lesson: Neither can children. Cain, the world's very first child, was so determined to be the world's first *only* child, he killed his brother Abel. Of course, the reason this peevish outburst occurred is because Adam and Eve allowed a third-party interloper to intrude in the raising of their children—never a good idea. That meddlesome protagonist was not the gossipy snake, but its Creator. I am speaking, of course, of God, who shows an alarming inclination to abet the killing of sons throughout the Bible. Just ask Abraham. Or Jesus.

So close to Jesus,

He sent my dreadful mother-in-law to Hell—and she wasn't even dead yet.

SURVIVALTIP When dropping into conversation "My children were stoned," ensure that you are not lamenting a current substance-abuse disciplinary problem, but simply bragging about the successful conclusion of all such disciplinary problems.

You see, Cain and Abel each gave God a gift. The Lord, showing deplorable manners even for such a primitive time, churlishly told Cain that his gift was not nearly good enough (Genesis 4:5) and He was going to take it back for store credit. Cain, rebuffed for his rushed gift selection, went away in a rage. After all, no one wants to go down in history as the world's first bad shopper. As a result of the jealousy inspired by God's rather ungrateful response to Cain's gift, Cain killed the brother who showed an uncanny knack for picking out the perfect little something to please even the most demanding—God. Truly, what do you buy the guy who made everything? Well, it

can't have left either Adam or Eve feeling too comfortable to know that there was a killer in the house. I imagine that this unease was aggravated when they took a moment to contemplate the dearth of options Cain had when it came time to decide whom to kill next.

in biblical times, the desire to "leave a good impression" was not meant metaphorically

When it came to correcting children in the Bible, no one spared the rod. Hence the expression "child rearing." I doubt this corporal contact was instigated out of any genuine fear of actually spoiling a child, but because children in ancient times tended not to have their own lawyers. Indeed, it would seem to me that the chance of successfully spoiling a child who spent each day trying to find enough food to live to see the next one (and avoiding the wavering path of myopic relatives, since no one had glasses) seems rather remote.

Nowadays, outside of seedy homosexual leather bars, Americans tend to ignore the Old Testament precepts of discipline. Social flaws are overlooked and behavior verily screaming for the welt of a rod, if not the cranial collapse of a rock, is left unchecked and encouraged. The result? I find myself in a society full of people left living for far too long not to render themselves an acute annoyance to me. A simple visit to any place open to the public leaves the observant hankering for a well-catered stoning.

Children are like fresh fruit. They have no taste when they are small and new; they should be thrown out when they turn rotten.

epistle of profound and compassionate christian advice: *does god watch us masturbate?*

> Dear Mrs. Bowers:
> Sometimes when I am alone at night, I touch myself in an impure way. I seem to have no control. I want to stop because God and Jesus don't like it, but I can't! How can you help me?
> Timmy, age 14

FROM THE LOUIS QUINZE DESK OF

Betty Bowers

AMERICA'S BEST CHRISTIAN

Dear Sweet Sullied Child of Christ:

Remember, next time you are about to cinch down your little BVDs to delight in the Satanic pleasures of the flesh, that while Mommy and Daddy may not hear your little adolescent moans, everyone in Heaven can. You see, every single person in Heaven can and does watch everything you do! Dead Grandpa! Dead Great-grandma! And all your dead pets!

They all know if you succumb to the impurities of carnal delight—and whether you wash your hands after using the rest room. If for any reason the knowledge that you are being watched heightens your pleasure, then you are wholly given over to Satan, and there is nothing I can do to help you at this point.

So close to Jesus, He brings people back from the dead just so I can have the last word,

america's first lady sits down for a lovely chat about family and fashion with america's best christian

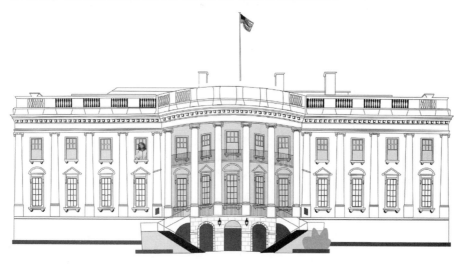

LAURA: Sanka?

BETTY: Actually, I'd prefer *real* coffee, dear.

LAURA: Oh, I'm sorry, Betty. We don't *do* caffeine.

BETTY: With Jenna, Barbara, and George in the family? I'd have thought you'd always have a fresh pot brewing "just in case."

LAURA: I don't know what you mean, Betty.

BETTY: Oh, Laura. Really! Save that supercilious look for the press. Everyone knows it's all the rage at college campuses to play W.W.J.D.

LAURA: I think that is wonderful. I always ask myself, when toying with taking just one more Xanax before bed, "What would Jesus do?" He always surprises me by doing two—

BETTY: They're not playing "What would Jesus do?" They're playing "What would Jenna drink?" It's disgraceful! And don't tell me George doesn't still knock them back in the private residence, Laura! Do you honestly think we in God's Own Party would select someone who slaughters syntax like that when they are sober? Anyway, I'd love to chat about your husband's shortcomings, but I'm always wary of venturing into potentially interminable subjects. Besides, we clearly have a potential emergency on our hands.

LAURA: What's happened?

95

BETTY: Your clothes.

LAURA: But I dressed like this at the governor's mansion.

BETTY: Living in Texas, you enjoyed the giddy license that comes with being unfettered by taste. You're in D.C. now. You need a designer.

LAURA: I used Michael Faircloth.

BETTY: Michael Faircloth? I don't know that house. I certainly don't recall seeing his showings in Paris, much less Milan, dear.

LAURA: He's from Yoakum, Texas, Betty. He designed the Dallas cheerleaders' outfits!

BETTY: Oh, dear. Who would have thought it possible to stand out for vulgarity in Texas? I knew we were in trouble even before the inauguration when you showed up to have lunch with Hillary Clinton in that horrid purple plaid suit!

LAURA: That is one of my favorite Butterick patterns, Betty! Besides, you were the one who told me to go for a Barneys suit.

BETTY: I meant the department store, not the *dinosaur*. Honestly, Laura, to look frumpy next to a woman who wears pastel pantsuits and has ankles like a Clydesdale takes enormous calculation. And just look at you now! While the Lord singled you out for an ample bosom, He gave all of us gravity, dear.

LAURA: I find a bra is often a little formal for day. It's a whole lot easier to just tuck my breasts into the elastic waistband of my Dress Barn skirt—otherwise I get a black eye when I gallop through the West Wing.

BETTY: Well, you wear suits that make you look like a stewardess for Aeroflot, dear. I don't understand it. I told you to pick a movie star and model your look after her.

LAURA: I did, Betty.

BETTY: Who?

LAURA: Lotte Lenya!

BETTY: Oh, I give up! How are your causes going?

LAURA: Well, since I am a teacher—

BETTY: One can only hope your learning techniques have been more successful *out-side* of the home, dear. I mean, honestly, how long can you trot that "I'm a teacher" chestnut out? You haven't taught since the invention of Post-its—and you speak as if the most eloquent book you ever read could fit on one!

LAURA: I'll overlook that.

BETTY: I hardly feel singled out. No doubt, with George in the house, you've spent most of your adult life *overlooking* things.

LAURA: Well, it is a skill that is certainly coming in very handy this afternoon, I must say. Anyway, I really want to promote reading, Betty.

BETTY: What is your favorite book?

LAURA: I absolutely love *Crime and Punishment.*

BETTY: Yes, well, in your household that concept is probably best left on the bookshelf—or you'd never see your husband or girls, dear. Besides, the correct answer was the Bible—whether you believe it or not. Remember that next time you are asked that question in front of a live mike.

LAURA: I also like Dostoyevsky's *The Brothers Karamazov.*

BETTY: I find its treatment of Jesus suspicious at best, dear, and your attachment to it alarming. Speaking of shocking habits when it comes to books, did you really Dewey-decimalize your entire private library, as I read in the paper?

LAURA: Yes. Some may find that a bit anal—

BETTY: Coming from a woman who Cloroxes everything from bras to bookshelves? No, that's not anal. That's anal-*compulsive,* dear. There is a difference. Let's talk about one of life's most important issues: hair. Hillary Clinton had more hairstyles than Alec Baldwin's back, but you seem to have stuck with a decidedly seventies do.

LAURA: What do you mean?

BETTY: Well, your coif was clearly inspired by one of the Osmond brothers. If Donny can change his, surely you can, too, dear. Besides, someone should have told you by now that our Republican distaste for mixing colors applies only to cars and races—not hair. Get some highlights. And, Laura, please stop smoking!

LAURA: What made you think I smoke?

BETTY: Your lips, dear. Either you smoke like a steel mill or you give collagen like most people give blood! Oh, and while I'm thinking about it, here is the card for the dear Jewish plastic surgeon in New York who does my freshening. Honestly, dear, you need to find someone who doesn't approach the task as if they were simply hanging wallpaper. One more cut-rate lift like that and people are going to think our First Lady is Chairman Mao! Now, let's talk about something important. Where am I going to sit at the dinner?

LAURA: Well, since you are America's best Christian, I was going to seat you right in between Ralph Reed and Mr. Falwell.

BETTY: Oh, wonderful. So I can spend the evening listening to that effeminate, nasal whine coming from someone in a booster chair on one side of me and the incessant slurping of gravy on the other side of me. Honestly, Jerry

may purport to follow Jesus, but when presented with a buffet, he's clearly begun to ask himself "What would Buddha do?" I don't think so, Laura. And don't seat me next to your girls. They were both sneaking gulps from my wine-glass last time. Honestly, it was filled so often, the staff must have thought Betty Ford was back in the house!

LAURA: Well, at least they weren't slamming your glass on the top of their heads every time they drained it like they did to the ambassador from Paraguay. That's why we don't usually have Jenna and–ah–um–well, the other one in the house. Not that family isn't important to me. In fact, when we were campaigning, I spent about 250 nights away from the girls during their last year of high school to go to other cities and tell folks how important my family is to me.

BETTY: Well, I can hardly blame you for fleeing, dear. They seem like quite a handful.

LAURA: Betty, I'll tell you, nothing demands more of any passive-aggressive woman's attention than rebellious children–unless, of course, you have an under-achiever husband with an addictive personality who got enormous pressure from his overbearing mother to get elected president.

BETTY: Well, the girls are certainly their father's children, dear. After all, George is no stranger to booze.

LAURA: George has been great with the girls. Before they went off to college, he sat down with Jenna and, uh, the one not going to school in Texas and told them that it is one thing to have "youthful indiscretions," but they can't use adoles-cence as an excuse forever. He reminded them that when a teenager gets to be around forty or fifty years old, it is probably time to cut back on the binge drinking and start using those cute little cocaine spoons for stirring amaretto Coffee-mate into your decaf.

BETTY: Well, there really is no justice, is there? I mean, George just drives around al-legedly hopped up on cocaine–doesn't kill anyone–and gets a ticket. And you run a stop sign and kill your boyfriend and get nothing. All I can say is the best thing about George being appointed president by the Supreme Court is that it will once again be safe for the rest of us to drive now that both of you are chauffeured wherever you go!

LAURA: I still feel awful about that killing.

BETTY: Well, look on the bright side, dear. Even if you drove around the Beltway for three weeks blindfolded at 145 miles per hour, given George's record in Texas, it's unlikely that you would ever catch up with your husband when it comes to killing people.

New York End Times

The only newspaper in America that is "Untouched by Unsaved Hands"

Heaven: low 70, high 71
Hell: 4,323°
Outlook: bleak

Betty Performs Amalfi Coast Miracle After a Lovely Lunch

POSITANO, ITALY (AP). While vacationing with her two sons on the Amalfi Coast last week, American religious leader and businesswoman Betty Bowers treated locals and tourists alike to a bona fide miracle. Mrs. Sol Rubenstein of New York said, "I walked over to her to see if all the diamonds on her Gucci sunglasses were real. I was amazed when she said they were because there must have been about forty karats worth. But she just said, 'Aren't they just the *kickiest?*'"

It was right after this exchange that Mrs. Rubenstein said the miracle occurred. One of Mrs. Bowers' buff and cut sons came running up from the sea, his swim trunks wet and clinging to his hard body, leaving nothing to the imagination. "He looked like something from one of those Abercrombie & Fitch catalogs," Mrs. Rubenstein breathlessly recounted. "I couldn't keep my eyes off his abs! Anyway, he complained that the Mediterranean was like a big pond because there was no surf. So, his mom puts her fabulous sunglasses into her bag—I could tell it was Bottega—and walks down to the water."

It was then that Mrs. Bowers is reported to have invoked the name of Jesus Christ. Waves worthy of the North Shore of Oahu immediately came crashing onto the pristine beach. Locals claimed they had never seen anything like it. When asked about the miracle, Mrs. Bowers demurred: "Miracle? Now, if you want to talk about my flawless skin tone—*that's* a miracle! Dear, if a woman can't call in a few chits with her Personal Savior to ensure her sons have a lovely vacation, what kind of mother would she be? Naturally, I do regret the loss of those five or six fishing villages down the coast, but it is not ours to question the Lord's will. Besides, the boys had a lovely time."

As a True Christian™, I would never question the wisdom of God trifurcating into the Trinity like a celestial stock split. Nevertheless, having three gods can tax the talents of even the most accomplished hostess in prayer. After all, a lady always likes to give her undivided attention. Fortunately, They don't require a quorum for requests involving less than $100,000.

epistle of profound and compassionate christian advice:
spare a heavy bible, spoil the child

> Dear Betty:
> As a Christian, I don't believe in sparing the rod. I have also found that a hard whack with my fifteen-pound Bible makes both a metaphysical and physical statement to my unruly children. But lately, I've been getting intrusive questions from their school headmaster about marks on their thighs. How can I assault my children with the Good Book without leaving visible marks that their prying teachers might see?
> Yours in the Blood,
> Anne McGuirk,
> Association of Irish Pro-Lifers

FROM THE LOUIS QUINZE DESK OF

Betty Bowers

AMERICA'S BEST CHRISTIAN

Dear Hellbound Sinner:
Simply read it to them, dear.
So close to Jesus, I've asked Him to stop eating so much garlic,

betty's guide to christlike family values

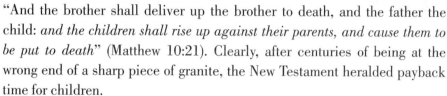

Leave No Stone Unthrown

Christ-like family values recognizes the shift in the balance of familial power represented by the New, more egalitarian, Testament. Whereas in the Old Testament, it was the parents who held all the ammunition, the New Testament encourages children faced with a family squabble not to overlook the rather effective strategy of mutually assured destruction. "And the brother shall deliver up the brother to death, and the father the child: *and the children shall rise up against their parents, and cause them to be put to death*" (Matthew 10:21). Clearly, after centuries of being at the wrong end of a sharp piece of granite, the New Testament heralded payback time for children.

Only Confirmed Bachelors Go to Heaven

I am always a little surprised with the preoccupation by lesser Christians with traditional family values. After all, shouldn't we be more concerned with *Christian* family values? Perhaps most so-called Christians eschew the New Testament's familial suggestions because they are, frankly, so shocking. For example, look at the two most important voices that differentiate our True Faith from Judaism: Jesus and the Apostle Paul. I note with mild suspicion that neither of them was married. Indeed, both of them told the rest of us never to marry (I Corinthians 7:8; Luke 20:34–35)! So much for the "sanctity of marriage"! Fortunately, this very un-American admonition has fallen on deaf ears—outside of homosexual enclaves like Manhattan, Disney, and the Vatican.

Love Your Neighbor, but Hate Your Family

While ignoring Jesus' requests (e.g., "give away your worldly possessions") is a basic precept of American Christian Fundamentalism, it makes for a refreshing change actually to do as He asks once in a while. Toward this end, and because I don't happen to get along with my dreadful mother-in-law,

I am bringing back into style one of the few things Christ asked us to do if we are to follow Him: *Hate our family.* Indeed, Jesus told prospective followers: "If any man come to me, and hate not his father, and mother, and wife, and children, and brethren, and sisters, yea, and his own life also, he cannot be my disciple" (Luke 14:26). I hasten to caution Jesus that questions arising from this peculiar interviewing criterion may violate hiring laws in numerous jurisdictions.

SURVIVALTIP Let's face it, hating your family has always been easy, but isn't it comforting to know that it is downright Christlike? Take a tip from Jesus: If your father has just died, don't squander the weekend on a depressing funeral (or even a laborious burial). Instead, go out with a pack of your always-present male friends! And if your mother dares to complain, use Jesus' rather callous quip from Matthew 8:22 that is sure to leave her speechless: "[*Snap!*] Let the dead bury the dead, girlfriend!"

Some have argued that Jesus just wanted people to hate their family "compared to their love of Jesus." Such ignorant people need to crack the spine on their Bible before God does likewise to their spines in Hell. Jesus did not talk about *relative* relative animosity, but absolute discord. He said, "For I am come to set a man at variance against his father, and the daughter against her mother, and the daughter-in-law against her mother-in-law" (Matthew 10:34). Notice, being a good Jewish boy and cognizant of Mary always lurking nearby, He did not say anything about turning a son against his mother.

Abandon Your Family–Win a Valuable Prize!

While American domestic relations courts have recently heeded the secular request to penalize so-called "deadbeat dads" in this life, God will more than make up for this pecuniary inconvenience in the next life. Jesus was quite clear in saying that the abandonment of your family will ensure fabulous riches in Heaven. "And every one that hath forsaken houses, or brethren, or sisters, or father, or mother, or wife, or children, or lands, for my name's sake, shall receive an hundredfold,* and shall inherit everlasting life" (Matthew 19:29). For those fathers contemplating running off to Hawaii with the house equity, it is important to bear in mind that not only is a guaranteed "hundredfold" a worthy return on their investment, "everlasting life" is beyond the jurisdiction of earthly domestic courts.

*This investment information provided by the Lord is only for your general information and use and is not intended to address your particular requirements. It is based on a good faith guesstimate by the Lord. In particular, the information does not constitute any form of advice or recommendation by the Lord and is not intended to be relied upon by sinners in making (or refraining from making) any specific investment or other decisions that affect salvation. Appropriate independent advice should be obtained before making any such decision. Any arrangement made between you and any third party not expressly mentioned in the Bible is at your sole risk and responsibility. For your information the Almighty would like to draw your attention to the following investment warnings. The price of units, funds, and the income derived from any investment can go down as well as up, and Christians may not get back the amount they invested, much less "an hundredfold." Past performance is not necessarily a guide to future performance (just watch VH1's *Behind the Music*).

epistle of profound and compassionate christian advice:
an open mind is the devil's playground

Dearest Betty:

I'm having a problem with one of my younger boys for which I seek your help. The other day, Matthew had the audacity to say he didn't understand how the story of Noah's Ark could actually be true. Needless to say, I beat that child until he recanted his skepticism and assured me it would never happen again. I explained to him that when we question God's Word, we are playing right into Satan's hands. The Devil views an open mind as an invitation to enter our lives and manipulate our thoughts.

As we all know, God has always been subject to volatile mood swings, largely instigated by the imperfections He made inherent in us all. During one particularly bad mood, God decided to brutally kill every man, woman, and child on Earth, except Noah and his family, through massive flooding and consequent drowning. To perpetuate life, He ordered Noah to build an ark and maintain a male and a female from every animal species on the ark.

Matthew pointed out that there are over a hundred million different species, ranging in size from elephants to insects. Since the Bible says Noah loaded the ark in a single day, Matthew argues that Noah would have to have boarded an average of 1,157 animals every second.

Again, I know this is foolish skepticism on my son's part, but I eagerly await Jesus' reply.

Your brother in Christ,

Harry Hardwick

Dear Brother Harry:

I must say that I find it very peevish of your child to be questioning Noah's efforts—a man so dutiful in fulfilling our dear Lord's wildly demanding wishes that he went to the trouble of going to a place that didn't even exist yet (i.e., Australia) to ensure that those adorable koala bears were saved from God's rather fickle love for His creations. Remind that thankless son of yours that if it weren't for Noah taking the time to line up all the billions of species, including all the AKA recognized breeds, Matthew wouldn't even have a little springer spaniel to play with. And how does he repay Noah's efforts? With intellectual inquiry. Such outrageous ingratitude!

If an open mind is the Devil's picnic, an intellectual outlook is the Devil's all-you-can-stomach buffet. This is why our faith has a glorious and, I must add, successful tradition of sweetening the theological pot to make the less blindly faithful obey. I am, of course, referring to acute physical pain. While the Catholic Church certainly can be credited with perfecting corporal "incentives" to faithfulness during their rather successful road show, known generally as the Inquisition, we Protestants have proven quite adept at conjuring our own painful persuasions against intrusive questions (see, for example, the old "board piled with stones" parlor game invented by American Fundamentalists' resourceful forefathers, the Puritans).

Why should the rules be any different when it is a child asking the impertinent? Even God tells us "spare the rod, spoil the child." And these are not idle words, coming from Someone who crucified His only Son. Even a cursory reading of the Bible reveals that our Lord has little time or patience for children. He slaughters them with the ease of someone eating potato chips.*

The Blessed Lord also does not suffer impertinent inquiry. For example, He turned Moses' sister into a leper just for asking a question that rubbed Him the wrong way (Numbers 12:1–9). So, I think you are on perfectly solid theological ground in beating the stuffing out of a child who asks an incisive question that makes the Bible look either ridiculous or wrong. Since we Fundamentalists have decided that every word in the Bible is God's, we can't turn back now or appear to waver in the face of logic, another tool of Satan. Even though the Bible is filled with outrageous absurdities and contradictions, it is imperative that your child be taught immediately to gloss over all of that and simply learn the mantra "God writes stuff that is so crazy only He can make sense of it."

If this doesn't work, do as you see fit. But remember that the secular laws regarding child rearing have strayed from God's law since the time of Abraham.

So close to Jesus, He not only washes my feet, He shaves my legs while we gossip about Mary,

Betty Bowers

---

*God drowns all children on Earth, except that smarmy Noah family (Genesis 7:23); God kills all firstborns in Egypt (Exodus 12:29); God murders an innocent child (I Samuel 15:3); God has bears kill forty-two kids for teasing a bald man (II Kings 2:23–24); God slaughters children for the mistakes of their father (Isaiah 14:21–22); God orders the slaughter of women and little children (Ezekiel 9:6), etc., etc., etc. Surely you get the idea by now, dear.

Betty's World-Famous "Brutal Death of Our Savior" Cookie Recipe

Gals, I have just the thing to turn the simple act of baking cookies into an opportunity to teach your children just how sinful and wretched they are in God's eyes!

You will need:

1 cup whole pecans	Ziploc bag
A gallon jug of very inexpensive vinegar	Wooden spoon
3 egg whites	Tape
Lots of salt	A KJV Bible (Do *not* substitute!)
1 cup sugar	

Have your domestic help (preferably one who speaks some form of English) preheat your custom-made stainless steel professional-quality oven to 300 degrees. (If you don't have help, get some.)

Place pecans in Ziploc bag and let children beat them with the wooden spoon, while screaming foul words of derision, to break pecans into small pieces. Explain that after Jesus was arrested, and before the Jews killed him, Roman soldiers beat Him just like they are beating those helpless pecans. Read John 19:1–3.

Put 1 teaspoon of vinegar into mixing bowl. Let each child smell the inexpensive vinegar. Explain that when Jesus was thirsty on the cross, he was given vinegar to drink. If they dare to ask, "Well, why didn't he just turn it into a nice chardonnay?" fill a tumbler with vinegar and say, "Here's your chardonnay, you little smart aleck!" If they complain, ask them, "Do you as a sinful little nobody deserve better than Jesus?" Read John 19:28–30.

Add egg whites to vinegar. Tell the children that white was the color of Jesus' skin—and generally the best color to be (unless you are Mrs. Bowers' shoes) when passing a police car. Explain that the meringue symbolizes the soft fluffy clouds in heaven that your children, as wretched sinners, have little chance of ever actually seeing. Read John 10:10–11.

Sprinkle a little salt into each child's hand. Make them eat it and brush the rest into the bowl. Explain that this represents the salty tears shed by Jesus' followers, and the bitterness of the children's disgusting sins. Remind them just how impure they are and how undeserving they are of His love—or your cookies! Read Luke 23:27.

So far, the ingredients have not been very appetizing and the children may be feeling rather queasy. Add 1 cup sugar. Explain that the sweetest part of the story is that God loves us so much that He killed Himself for us. Don't let them ask a lot of follow-up questions as, frankly, this all gets a little hard to explain—just brandish the vinegar if things get tricky. Read Psalms 34:8 and John 3:16.

Beat with a mixer on high speed and fold in broken nuts. Drop by teaspoons onto wax-paper-covered cookie sheet. Explain that each mound represents the rocky tomb where Jesus' body was laid. Remind them that if Jesus was buried in a hole, they as vile sinners deserve to be thrown out into the road to be pecked to death by crows and run over by minivans. Read Matthew 27:57–60.

Put the cookie sheet in the oven, close the door, and turn the oven off.

Give each child a piece of tape and seal the oven door. Explain that Jesus' tomb was sealed, cutting off His last bit of oxygen so that He would have quickly suffocated. Like the Jews, they, too, are now responsible for killing Jesus. Read Matthew 27:65–66.

Send your children to bed, telling them they will be sad to be without the cookies, just as a handful of people in the Bible seemed to be somewhat gloomy over being without Jesus.

After about an hour, uncork a lovely, unassuming wine and open the oven. The cookies are wonderful with a flinty chardonnay. You won't stop until you've had them all. Glory!

When your children come downstairs in the morning, they will discover that the oven door has been ripped open and all the cookies have disappeared. Remind them that this is exactly what happened when Jesus' followers returned to the tomb and found Him gone—only, after three days, that tomb probably didn't smell nearly as fragrant as your oven!

If your children cry because they didn't get any cookies, remind that they are worthless sinners who deserve to be tortured in Hell and since their sins killed Jesus, they don't deserve treats. Read Matthew 28:1–9.

WWBW?

What Would Betty Wear?

a look of humble self-sacrifice—and an $8,000 prada jacket!

Since the rather gothic Catholics think they are actually eating the flesh and blood of Jesus at communion, I wonder if there is room in their pews for vegans? I do have it from reliable, if not reputable, Catholic sources that the blood of Christ tends to be light in tannins with a blackberry-tobacco finish. It really calls for a strong cheese (try Stilton) instead of a wan bread that tastes like Styrofoam!

epistle of profound and compassionate christian advice:
wearing execution devices as jewelry

Dear Mrs. Bowers:

For many years now I have worn a gold cross around my neck, and it is a source of constant inspiration and strength for me and those who see it. But recently I have been thinking of changing to one featuring the body of Jesus crucified on it. Is this vanity, or is it the Lord suggesting that I should upgrade my cross for the sake of myself and others?

Yours sincerely,
Lillian Push

FROM THE LOUIS QUINZE DESK OF

Betty Bowers

AMERICA'S BEST CHRISTIAN

Dear Mrs. Push:

The ineffable nuances that separate jewelry that most woman wear from what Mrs. Bowers would be seen with is a subject almost as close to me as Jesus. Indeed, if you ever hear me refer to being "stoned to death," I have usually just returned from a joyous afternoon in the private viewing room at Cartier.

One of the great lessons of life is that if one is resourceful enough, everything can be parlayed into a reason for quality jewelry. Religion is certainly no exception. Regrettably, the focal design of our particular religion happens to be a device of state-sanctioned human execution. Not what I would have chosen, but we are left by God to work with it. It does, however, give me some pause for relief that Jesus did not wait until twenty-first-century America to visit, as electric chairs and lethal injection apparatus are rather difficult to evoke with any elegance—even made of platinum.

Now, to your question. Should one wear a lavaliere that depicts a human body in the process of being tortured to death? The answer would appear self-evident to all but Marilyn Manson fans and Catholics. For my taste, while a simple cross coyly alludes to torture, anything more graphic seems to morbidly delight in the specifics and generally ruin the geometric pleasures of the unadorned cross. In any event, jewelry that depicts anyone in the act of actually dying an agonizing death would seem incontrovertibly too gothic to be worn by anyone other than Cher before 5:00 P.M.

So close to Jesus, we file joint 1040s,

Betty Bowers

protect the environment from visual pollution: encourage the poorly dressed to stay home

Anyone taking as long a look as they can bear at our nation's populace will arrive at only one conclusion: There are quite clearly not enough shut-ins in this country. When people are thoughtless enough to smoke in a public place, they are usually met with a wild-eyed tizzy over the second-hand smoke. But no one seems to raise a penciled eyebrow, much less a stern voice, when someone's egregious choice of fabric for a blouse assaults our eyes with secondhand visual pollution.

After several months of careful observation, and a lovely private trip through Versailles, I finally realized the root of the problem. Most of the living are already experiencing a Hell of their own each time they encounter a full-length mirror. Regrettably, from the looks of most of them, such encounters are far too rare indeed. With this in mind, Bringing Integrity To Christian Homemakers has launched its Full-Length Mirror Drive to make sure that one reasonably long mirror (that will remind Americans to actually look at their shoes) will be in every home and/or trailer by next year. While access to such mirrors may not cause some of the more egregious dressers to buy lovely new things, it will, hopefully, provide them incentive to resort to having all their meals and clothing delivered. Praise the Lord when that glorious day arrives!

So close to Jesus,

we always sing "I Got You Babe" together at karaoke.

Biblical Shopping Tip: Did you know that there are only 257 shopping days until the Apocalypse? Shopping during the End Times carries the burden of knowing that each gift you give will be your last chance to make a good impression. Also, returns will be difficult once the Almighty has turned every store into a smoldering ruin. But there is a bright side—it's not as if American Express can forward your enormous bill to God's glory!

Evolution is clearly a lie. After all, if we have supposedly descended from Neanderthals, why are they still living in Mississippi?

epistle of profound and compassionate christian advice:
what should a christian lady wear to an abortion-clinic bombing?

Dear Mrs. Betty Bowers,

I am in desperate need of your divinely inspired advice. I know all too well the importance of the proper apparel for every occasion, but I just never seem to have your blessed fashion sense. For instance, what do you suggest for abortion-clinic bombings? I always seem to be overdressed.

Desperate and Dowdy in Dallas

Dear Dowdy in Dallas (and, let's face it, who isn't?):

On the advice of in-house counsel, I cannot divulge what I may (or may not) have worn to certain abortion-clinic bombings, but as someone who has spent countless hours in abortion-clinic protests, I think I speak with some authority on the appropriate attire for such occasions. First of all, *never* take your fashion cues from those around you. While I won't say an unkind word about my fellow Sisters in Christ, an unkind word about their wardrobe is unavoidable. Denim and poly-cotton tees with strenuously cheerful aphorisms are best kept for dusting the trailer—and a cardigan collection with an overbearing knit for each bank holiday is best left to my Sister-in-Christ Patsy Ramsey, dear.

Make it your goal to be the most fabulously turned out when the tear gas falls! There is a reason for this beyond simply showing up other women (as if that weren't enough!). If you're wearing a lovely three-ply silk A-line Calvin Klein camel suit, no one will think twice if you say, "I'm sorry, I simply cannot get down on the ground in THIS!" If you are wearing lovely cultured pearl bracelets, no one will balk when you say, "I simply cannot put myself in a position where I might be handcuffed with THESE!" If you are wearing a plush Dolce & Gabbana cashmere coat, no one will look askance when you say, "I simply cannot climb into that filthy police car in THIS!"

Now, for life's biggest question: Heel size. Some would argue for a "sensible heel." Au contraire! Wear the longest, pointiest heel you own. That way, if one of those vile abortionists hits the ground, you will have something to grind into her face. As you are not going to get on the ground, be handcuffed, or climb into a squad car, it is the least you can do to help!

So close to Jesus, there's talk of a Holy Quadrangle,

a day in the life of america's best christian: *knowing which designers and heel size are most pleasing to the lord*

10:16 A.M., Landover Baptist Church

The flight on my ministry Gulfstream to Landover Baptist took less time than usual, so I ordered the pilot to do my signature crucifix formation approach over the chapel before landing. This allowed the congregation gathering on the steps to know that America's most saved Baptist would be attending this morning's service. Sometimes, there is no harm in giving clothed people something to get excited about. Many people ask me why we fly most weeks to Iowa for church. The reason is rather obvious. Landover Baptist is simply the most conservative church in America that doesn't involve handling snakes or wearing machine-washable fabrics.

As I walked down the chapel aisle, I signaled for Mr. Bowers to remove my Gucci coat. I think it selfish not to allow the congregation an opportunity to witness what a stylish ensemble actually looks like. Since my beloved Brothers and Sisters in Christ live in Iowa, I am their only opportunity to view what is fashionable *while it still is*. I regally, yet without a trace of hauteur, walked to the front of the 12,500-seat church. I pretended not to see all the Tin-Wing Tithers in the $50 seats who were trying to get my attention—not because I didn't wish to be polite, but because the cut of this particular dress didn't lend itself to overt waving. When I arrived at my reserved pew, I noticed poor Sister-in-Christ Taffy with hair so dark and high she gave the appearance of having just single-handedly changed the guard at Buckingham Palace. I acknowledged her with a lovely smile and conscientiously replicated the compliment I had given her stridently floral dress the last several times I had seen it: "What an aggressive choice, dear." I then signaled to Pastor Deacon Fred by snapping my Fabergé compact shut that we were ready for the service to begin.

epistle of profound and compassionate christian advice:
what does a christian lady wear to a stylish execution?

Do you lack that certain *je ne sais coif* favored by our Lord because you color your own hair? Remember: the only thing unforgiving about Heaven is its lighting!

Dear Betty:

The other day, Harry and I took our two youngest children to their first execution. Now, Hubby and I have been to many without the children, of course. In fact, one of the security guards at the Freehold penitentiary once jokingly asked us if we had season tickets. From the oversize wired chair with the metal hat, to the hissing sound of colorless gas, to the sparkling tip of a freshly cleaned syringe, we've experienced it all. Oh, the memories. Glory!

A problem arose this time, though, because the prisoner was white and he was being executed for killing a colored person. We tried to find out which shade, but it remains a mystery. Well, once I saw that it was a white person going to be killed, I must admit that I was completely thrown off. You see, I always try to pick an outfit that complements not only my skin tone, but also that of the condemned. As these shades have historically been at opposite ends of the spectrum, it has afforded me a wide latitude (no comment about my recent weight gain, Betty!) in selecting the palette for my outfit.

I am not going to reproach myself for my lack of forethought for, truly, who would have guessed such an unusual event would occur? What should I have worn? My seal coat?

In the Blood,
Heather

FROM THE LOUIS QUINZE DESK OF

Betty Bowers

AMERICA'S BEST CHRISTIAN

Dear Sister-in-Christ Heather:

Truly, it is becoming so difficult to plan suitable entertainment for our Christian children in a secular world with shifting values. Here you looked forward to a lovely day of catered retribution in hopes of providing your children with a lesson about what happens to people of color when they rub American juries the wrong way, only to have it ruined by the cagey vicissitudes of the American justice system.

Dressing for an execution is a delicate task that requires an abundance of nuance and tulle. When you enter your walk-in closet, veer toward cheerful colors and busy fabrics. If you carelessly grab a hanger with anything even remotely somber, spectators might assume that you are connected socially with the type of trash who always winds up executed. Thus, black needs to be worn with caution and aplomb—and should always be accessorized with an unambiguous smile calibrated to be just shy of gloating.

A good rule of thumb in dressing for an execution is to treat it as a wedding and the executed as the bride. While it is, of course, almost impossible, it is important not to *try* to show up the person who is about to be killed. After all, dear, it is *his* day. Find out what color he will be killed in and avoid it. Out of caution, steer clear of stripes and orange. The soon-to-be-killed will appreciate you for these thoughtful touches that allow him to feel unique on this very important day in his soon-to-be-over life. Allow him to begin his decent into the fiery pits of Hell feeling special. It is the least we can do, as Christians, before we kill him.

Let's talk about chapeaux for a moment. Out of consideration for those in the cheaper seats, I try not to wear a broad-brimmed hat. Unless, of course, the dress just demands it! Many eschew a veil, lest it be misconstrued as sympathy for the person who undoubtedly deserves to die. I disagree with this choice. A veil does not have to be black. Try a saucy red! And, besides, it is never a good idea for a Christian lady to give a clear view of her face when she is going to be in the company of criminals and their vindictive families. As for slipping on a seal coat, while wearing the pelts of an animal clubbed to death is a lovely metaphoric choice for the occasion, trust me, metaphoric fashion statements are often difficult to pull off, are likely to be misconstrued, and should therefore be left to me.

So close to Jesus, I always ask for a table for two when dining alone,

Betty Bowers

"It is a well-known fact that the lie-beral hoax of so-called global warming is due entirely to urban sprawl in Hell."
—Betty's graduation speech at Landover Baptist University for the Saved

from the diary of america's best christian: *speaking in tongues without a teleprompter*

11:35 A.M., Landover Baptist Church

About midway through services, the Holy Ghost moved me to begin speaking in tongues. As a Baptist, I normally refuse to engage in tongues, as I consider it to be a rather vulgar display best left to attention-seeking Pentecostals. Nevertheless, it is always awkward to say no to the Holy Ghost, especially when He is right there before me asking with that charming little dove smile of His.

The only ground rule I have imposed on the Holy Ghost is that whatever I say will always be clever and contain no malapropisms or obscenities. I am always pleased to note that, even though in the throes of religious rapture, I instinctively know which of Landover Baptist's five television cameras to address at all times. This morning, I was heartened to be told that the tongue the Holy Ghost had chosen for me, once again, was called English. I consider myself quite fortunate that the Holy Ghost has had me speak in perfect English ever since He moved me to speak in tongues three years ago. While there would be a certain glamour in unexpectedly breaking into French (I would insist on a Tours accent), as Jacqueline Kennedy did to the delight of the normally ornery Parisians, back before she sold herself to the highest bidder, destabilizing the price of hookers from Athens to Anchorage, there was equal chance that one could also end up speaking an exotic Bali dialect and risk completely losing the house. When wearing silk, one should always avoid languages that employ alarming amounts of spittle.

WWBC?

What Would Betty Change?

homosexuals—and then into something shimmering for dinner!

baptists are saving homosexuals: the world's only fortune 500 ex-gay ministry

BASH has only two goals:

1. To prove to the world that the hobby of homosexuality is just a silly "choice."

2. To provide artistic husbands for women who become flummoxed when arranging flowers, picking complementary fabrics for lining drapes, choosing furniture or throw pillows, or who have historically ruined otherwise suitable outfits by slipping on the wrong pair of earrings.

Baptists Are Saving Homosexuals

Be a man, girl!

Ex-Gay Ministry

Last month, over twelve thousand degenerates desperate for respectability and comfortable domestic shoes paid $4,500 to join the ranks of my ex-gay ministry BASH. To this date, *tens* of BASH alumni have become so desissified that they are actually able to appear at public functions without scoffing at light fixtures or uttering the word "please" as a multisyllabic word. After four years of relentless reeducation, one ex-gay has even gotten to the point where he eventually thinks of Jesus' mother when someone whispers the word "Madonna." Praise the Lord!

BASH is turning the tithe on horribly arch gay boys, teaching them that an ability to discern subtle differences among 2,700 shades of tawny taupe

119

cannot alone be effectively parlayed into a godly existence. And BASH is using a method as old as religion itself—*coercive torture*. The therapy is ingenious! My assistant Miss Anne Thrope shows a series of regrettably graphic slides of sundry sexual acts to a roomful of hairdresser/florist types. When a slide depicts two (sometimes more!) men together, a 120-volt electric current (generated by a Hoover upright generously donated by Sister Taffy) is run through the men's genitalia. When the picture shows a normal Christian married couple engaged in natural procreative activities (fortunately for all involved, these slides are not visible, as the lights, of course, are never "on" when a Christian woman is undergoing the godly submission to the ungodly marital act), a score of girls from my Christian Crack Whore Ministry services the men as positive reinforcement.

So close to Jesus,
He's opened up to me about
His martyr complex.

Not only is the therapy working, the soon-to-be-heterosexual men involved are eager to undergo whatever torment is necessary to be just like us! Indeed, just last week, several of the men—especially those who wear leather jackets, pants, and hats—complained that the voltage was way too low. Truly, it brought tears of joy to my eyes to know that these men are so determined to change!

BASH ex-gay testimony: jesus gave me the one thing i always lacked: cachet!

Before finding Jesus, I would go out shopping and haul back bags of ill-conceived purchases for my wardrobe and coffee table. No more! For example, the other day I was at T. J. Maxx. I looked at a twice-marked-down putty-colored polo shirt (*real* Ralph Lauren!)—then back at the periwinkle. Which one to buy? I'd love to get both, but could barely afford one. Two would be sinful. So, I asked myself the question I always ask when facing an important moral dilemma: "What would Jesus do?" The answer came to me immediately. He would choose the putty! It had that deliciously discreet quality that wouldn't unnecessarily draw attention to the wearer—and "understated" is a tough look to pull off when you are a Supreme Being. Putty would also allow the Lord to mix without remark with both people He was bringing back to life and people He was damning to Hell—and versatility is an important aspect of any limited wardrobe.

I grabbed the lighter shirt and walked to the register with the sureness of step that comes only from knowing God regards you as a smart shopper. But just as I handed the sales clerk my putty polo, it hit me: What *would* Jesus do? Yes, He would do putty. Definitely. But only *before* the crucifixion. After the ascension, he would surely go for the more showy "look what I did" periwinkle. I then knew that He meant for me to have both. Isn't God good to us?

Since coming out of the homosexual lifestyle, I have come to rely upon Jesus for all my earthly decisions. When picking wallpaper for the guest powder room, I surveyed hundreds of samples at the Home Depot and asked myself, "What would Jesus do?" He surprised me by going with a gold-flocked number with red asexual cupids. Not something I would have chosen. But you should see how well it works with the red velveteen curtains He picked out for over the commode!

Finding Jesus has made my life is so much easier. When presented with several yummy specials at a restaurant, I always ask, "What would Jesus do?" before ordering, and I am *never* disappointed. Even though Jesus tends to eat a lot more red meat than I would care for (people who know they are never going to see forty tend not to worry about cholesterol!), He has an unerring sense for which vegetable colors most surprisingly complement the palette of the sauce. The only hitch is when it comes to ordering wine. Asking "What would Jesus do?" is of little assistance when the answer is always, "He'd make His own."

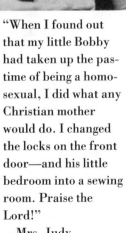

"When I found out that my little Bobby had taken up the pastime of being a homosexual, I did what any Christian mother would do. I changed the locks on the front door—and his little bedroom into a sewing room. Praise the Lord!"
—Mrs. Judy O'Christian

the homosexual agenda revealed!

As every True Christian™ knows, there is only one enemy that threatens our entire civilization. And I am, of course, talking about those damned homosexuals! Yes, they give otherwise dull hair radiant highlights and our imperfect décor those fabulous flourishes that elude our more predictable heterosexual sensibilities, but at what price? In exchange for a little panache, we allow homosexuals to steal our children and destroy our Christian marriages. And how do they do this? With their secret master plan—the Homosexual Agenda!

Up until now, the details of the Homosexual Agenda have been kept more secret than the nature of certain high-profile celebrity marriages. But I am pleased to announce that through innumerable free vodka sea breezes and some artful Christian skullduggery, I have gotten my hands on an authentic copy of the Homosexual Agenda. Never again shall we be surprised by what these malevolent nancy boys are up to. While they may still be able to surprise us with a cunningly perfect piece of Chinese porcelain for our Biedermeier end table, they will never again be able to deviously take over our culture, families and prime-time television without God-fearing Christians being one step ahead of them! Praise the Lord!

the homosexual agenda

8:00 A.M. Wake up. Wonder where you are.

8:01 A.M. Realize you are lying on 100 percent cotton sheets of at least a 300 thread count, so don't panic. At least you're not slumming.

8:02 A.M. Realize you are actually in your own bed *for a change.* Wake stranger next to you and tell him you are late for work so won't be able to cook breakfast for him. Mutter "sorry" as you help him look for his far-flung underwear. You find out that you tore his boxers while ripping them off him last night, so you "loan" him a pair of boxer briefs, but not the new 2x(ist) ones because you never intend to see him again.

8:05 A.M. Tell the stranger, whose name eludes you, "It was fun. I'll give you a call," as you usher him out the door, avoiding his egregious morning breath.

8:06 A.M. Crumple and dispose of the piece of paper with his telephone number on it when you get to the kitchen.

8:07 A.M. Make a protein shake while watching the *Today* show. Scoff at Matt Lauer. I mean, even *you* don't have the hips to pull off Jennifer Lopez for Halloween!

8:30 A.M. Italian or domestic? Decide to go with three-button Italian and the only shirt that is clean.

8:45 A.M. Climb into red BMW Z-3 and try not to look too much like Barbie driving one of her accessories as you pull out of your underground parking. Rēvos or Armanis? Go with Rēvos.

9:35 A.M. Stroll into office.

9:36 A.M. Close door to office and call best friend and laugh about the guy who spent the night at your condo. Point out something annoying about best friend's boyfriend but quickly add, "It doesn't matter what everyone else thinks, just as long as you love him."

10:15 A.M. Leave office, telling your secretary you are "meeting with a client." Pretend not to notice her insubordinate roll of her eyes (or the cloying "poem" she has tacked to her cubicle wall).

10:30 A.M. Have hair appointment for lowlights and cut you saw on someone ten years younger. Purchase Aveda Anti-Humectant Pomade even though you have no idea what it is supposed to do.

11:30 A.M. Run into personal trainer at gym. Pester him about getting you human growth hormone. Spend thirty minutes talking to friends on your cell phone while using Hammer Strength machines, preparing a mental matrix of which circuit parties everyone is going to and which are now passé.

12:00 P.M. Tan. Schedule back waxing in time for Saturday party where you know you will end up shirtless.

12:30 P.M. Pay trainer for anabolic steroids and schedule a workout. Shower, taking ten minutes to knot your tie while you check out your best friend's boyfriend undress with the calculation of someone used to wearing a t-back and having dollars stuffed in his crotch.

1:00 P.M. Meet for lunch at a hot, new restaurant someone for whom you know only his waist, chest, and penis size from AOL M4M chat. Because the maître d' recognizes you from the White Party, you are whisked past the Christian heterosexual couples who have been waiting patiently for a table since 12:30.

2:30 P.M. "Dessert at your place." Find out, once again, people lie on AOL.

3:33 P.M. Assume complete control of the U.S., state, and local governments (in addition to other nations' governments); destroy all healthy Christian marriages; recruit all children grades Kindergarten through 12 into your amoral, filthy lifestyle; secure complete control of the media, starting with sitcoms; molest innocent Boy Scouts; give AIDS to as many people as you can; host a pornographic "art" exhibit at your local art museum; and turn people away from Jesus, causing them to burn forever in Hell.

4:10 P.M. Time permitting, bring about the general decline of Western Civilization and look as if you are having way too much fun doing it.

4:30 P.M. Take a disco nap to prevent facial wrinkles from the stress of world conquest and being so terribly witty.

6:00 P.M. Open a fabulous new bottle of Malbec.

6:47 P.M. Bake Ketamine for weekend. Test recipe.

8:30 P.M. Enjoy light dinner with catty homosexual friends at a new restaurant you will be "over" by the time it gets its first review in the local paper.

10:30 P.M. Cocktails at a debauched gay bar, avoiding alcoholic queens who try to navigate a crowd with a lit cigarette in one hand and a Stoli in a cheap plastic cup in the other. As you pass by, loudly observe, "It's to stir the cocktail, *not* to drink through, Miss Fool."

12:00 A.M. "Nightcap at your place." Find out that people lie in bars, too.

It's nothing personal.
God told me to
hate you!

epistle of profound and compassionate christian advice:
one boy scout merit badge too far

Dear Mrs. Bowers:

One of the reasons I joined the Boy Scouts was I thought it would be safe from homos. Those perverts really annoy me since they are so shameless, they constantly run through my mind in various states of undress. Anyway, if that isn't bold enough, the other night on our overnight jamboree, I was very surprised when my best friend entered me from behind. Should I turn him in to my scout master?

David, Boy Scout

FROM THE LOUIS QUINZE DESK OF

Betty Bowers

AMERICA'S BEST CHRISTIAN

Dear Sodomite:

If the only thing you felt when someone put his penis up your behind was "surprise," I have a strong suspicion that you have done this before. As such, you are clearly lost to Satan.

So close to Jesus, the other two members of the Trinity refer to me as "Yoko Bowers,"

a day in the life of america's best christian: *cashing in your three-dollar bills*

4:16 P.M., Betty Bowers' Christian Ministries, Studio D

When I arrived at the studio for the broadcast of *The Bowers Hour,* my assistant Anne greeted me at the door. There was a problem. The first half hour of the program was devoted to a fund-raiser for my ex-gay ministry Baptists Are Saving Homosexuals. The money was earmarked for my homosexual outreach programs in Paris, Portofino, Monte Carlo, Lake Como, and the Amalfi Coast. I will say this: After countless years trying to convert effeminate urban gay boys into effeminate suburban husbands, I have learned that you may not actually be able to change someone's sexual orientation, but you can certainly make a lot of money trying. Praise the Lord!

Anyway, Anne was in a tizzy. You see, I was scheduled to do a scripted interview with BASH's most famous ex-gay Juan Balk. But Juan had disappeared. According to Anne, he had "lapsed" in makeup. Fifteen minutes to airtime and Juan had run off with Kevin, my makeup man. Naturally, the first thought that crossed my mind was who was going to do my face? I had to think fast.

As sometimes happens, the Lord provides in moments of need. Just as I was crossing the set in search of someone licensed to wield a makeup brush, I ran into my son Cliff.

When I looked at Cliff's Ford-model-handsome profile and beefy biceps, I thought, Who better to exemplify the potent allure of heterosexuality to fey creatures yearning to be free of the hobby of homosexuality? Unfortunately, Cliff was not particularly cooperative at first. He made some noise about not wanting to be my "ex-gay poster boy." I asked him, "Why not? Those gays have what I want—disposable income for tithing. And you have what they want—abs you could scallop potatoes on." Cliff rather meekly responded by telling me he wasn't gay. My response was quick and convincing: "See? BASH works! Praise the Lord!" He had to do his own makeup, which I thought turned out alarmingly well, only adding

verisimilitude to the portion of the script that mentioned he used to be a drag queen, but he was in the interview chair in ten minutes and read the TelePrompTer with élan. Indeed, with almost too much sincerity for my taste. Having to field one outraged wireless call from Mr. Bowers was certainly worth hearing all the contribution phones ringing like a frenzied carillon from the tiered phone banks behind us. Fortunately, I had the foresight to instruct the people manning the phones not to promise a meeting with Cliff to the scores of male callers for anything less than a pledge at the $1,000 level.

epistle of profound and compassionate christian advice:
does an ex-gay have to give up the fabulous gay clothes?

Dearest Betty:

As a new ex-gay, I'm finding it difficult to adopt the indicia of hetero-sexuality. I mean, I can learn to live without gorgeous guys with hot, hard chests to nestle my head in, but do I really have to wear extremely un-flattering jeans? Since I am no longer feeling attracted to beautiful boys with bulging triceps and pecs to die for (and that yummy trail of chest hair that beckons into their trousers), does that mean I must forsake all of my old gay fashion sensibilities about what makes a wardrobe work? Please help.

Urban Hetero but Not Suburban Retro

FROM THE LOUIS QUINZE DESK OF

Betty Bowers

AMERICA'S BEST CHRISTIAN

Dear Neo-Hetero Sinner:

As we all know, the decision to take up the hobby of being a homo-sexual is routinely made with no more care or attention than it takes most husbands to choose a tie. Once that reckless decision is made,

however, returning to a life of heterosexuality is thwart with tricky transitions. You simply cannot expect to be convincing as a newly minted heterosexual male overnight, dear. For example, while you may immediately replace your Diesel size 31 black jeans with Arizona brand size 36 kelly green active wear, it may take months before your bottom experiences structural failure and your stomach is sufficiently cantilevered over your belt to convincingly pull off your new wardrobe. (On a positive note, you will be pleased to find that one of the advantages of not dressing like a homosexual is that your belt will now often come free with your pants, which are now called "slacks.")

My recommendation is to start with a look that requires little skill and no taste. So you can either dress as a member of a boy band or as a golfer. Since I harbor significant doubts about most boy band members' ability to resist the pastime of being a homosexual, I think it is best that you send a less-ambiguous message and stick to golf clothing. Such apparel is designed so that it is virtually impossible to distinguish the most nattily dressed golfer from someone purposely trying to dress like a buffoon. Truly, when one makes the decision to dress as an Easter egg, it becomes too fine a point to quibble over whether one is inspired by Fabergé or Cadbury's. The complete absence of any taste that appears to be the very foundation to this "look" provides a certain license to err that is not normally found in fashion outside of German beer gardens.

You will find that your new wardrobe will serve as potent incentive not to look to lapse back into the homosexual lifestyle. For once you have acquired your new "hetero look," returning to a gay bar will not only lead to certain damnation, it will result in humiliating rejection.

So close to Jesus, I let Him use my cell phone if I have minutes left at the end of the month,

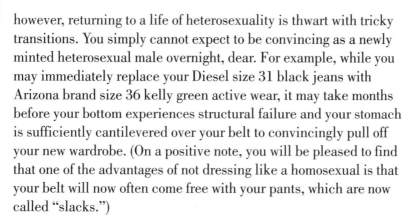

did your child wake up this morning and decide to be a homosexual?

BASH: Baptists Are Saving Homosexuals

is proud to introduce the world's FIRST ex-gay ministry for that willful under-10 set

Has your youngster decided to embrace the ungodly hobby of being a homosexual?

We all know that children are not "born gay." That is a lie from the very pit of a sulfurous Hell and, more important, a concept that plays havoc with our ability to block so-called antidiscrimination laws. As all True Christians™ know, some children simply wake up one morning and say to themselves: "I think I'm going to start acting like a flamboyant homosexual." Has your child begun to prance down this crooked road to Hell? Take BASH KIDS' simple True or False test to find out if your child is a candidate for heterosexual rehabilitation:

T ☐ F ☐ When you take your five-year-old son to look at the action figures at Toys "R" Us, does he gaze longingly at the Special Edition Jean Paul Gaultier Fabulous Manhattan Hostess Barbie, but scoff, "How outré for evening, Mommy! And that cut is so *Friends* two seasons ago!"

T ☐ F ☐ When your one-year-old boy first stands up, is it to perform a perfectly executed plié?

T ☐ F ☐ Does three-year-old Barbara convert her pink Barbie town house into a Meineke Muffler franchise?

T ❑ F ❑ Does two-year-old little Bobby crawl out of his Baby Gap denim overalls, only to show up for feedings wearing a smart cashmere sweater set and a simple strand of pearls?

T ❑ F ❑ Does your four-year-old little girl eschew dainty lace for corduroy and rewire the electrical outlets on your porch?

T ❑ F ❑ When you have dinner guests, does your eight-year-old boy climb out of his bunk bed, slip into something sequined, and slink down the staircase regaling your guests with a heart-rending, coquettish version of "The Man Who Got Away" like a four-foot, liquored-up Judy Garland?

T ❑ F ❑ Does Daddy's little princess pass up tulle for tools?

T ❑ F ❑ Does your six-year-old son shriek in ghastly apoplexy until you agree to wear Prada to the parent/teacher meeting?

T ❑ F ❑ Does your little boy keep throwing out all your silk floral arrangements while you are sleeping and calling reputable florists to have everything replaced with impeccably chosen exotic blooms that are new to you, but that he knows by name and scent?

T ❑ F ❑ When your little daughter utters her first word, does she talk like a sailor?

T ❑ F ❑ Does your eight-year-old boy complain that your pumps are sporting "last season's heel," that you look "too off-the-rack" or sneer that "not even hausfraus in Nebraska are wearing that tired Ralph Lauren fragrance"?

T ❑ F ❑ When cleaning out from under your little girl's bed, do you invariably find long-neck beer bottles and blue chalk for pool cues?

T ❑ F ❑ When you walk into the room wearing a new dress, does your husband barely notice, but your seven-year-old son breathlessly exclaims: "Cerise and aubergine! To die for, Mommy!"

T ❑ F ❑ When you take your children to Blockbuster, does your little girl cry if you don't rent *Personal Best,* or does your little boy try to shoplift the wide-screen version of *Funny Girl?*

WWBS?

what would betty shoot?

a look of unveiled reproof—and then a well-placed warning shot!

"All the News That Fits, We Print"

New York End Times

The only newspaper in America that is "Untouched by Unsaved Hands"

Heaven: low 70, high 71
Hell: 4,323°
Outlook: bleak

Unarmed Student Shot in the Head by a Jesus Puppet

FREEHOLD, IOWA (AP). A student at Landover Baptist Christian Pre-school was shot on Friday when a classmate's handgun went off during a biblical puppet show. After forty minutes of imprecatory prayer and a full investigation by Landover Baptist In-House Security, the child was rushed to Landover Baptist Pediatric Hospital for the Saved, where he was immediately pronounced "gone to Jesus." Harebrained Communist liberals immediately jumped on the incident as yet one more excuse to deprive Americans of the guns Jesus wants them to load and carry.

Appearing on CNN, Betty Bowers

was unapologetic. "All of our students are, of course, required to be armed at all times. And we have gone to great expense to protect our students from the unarmed. Indeed, the very latest metal detectors have been

---

installed at all entrances to our schools. If a detector doesn't 'beep,' we know the student is unarmed and unable to defend himself in a truly American manner—with bullets. He is, therefore, a security threat to his little classmates. I don't know how this so-called 'victim' was allowed to slip into class without a handgun to defend himself from the Jesus puppet, but I blame the parents."

The child's teacher, Veronica Woodchester, recalling the shooting, said: "The puppet show was going really well. We were recounting Old Testament wrath to the delight of the youngsters. Even though it was the Old Testament, we still had a Jesus puppet because we are Christian and I just felt like the whole thing would be way too *Jewish* without Him. Anyway, God was killing whole villages of firstborns, but the Jesus puppet went off-scripture and started shooting. It's the third student I've lost this semester, and it really makes me very, very angry. I mean, there is no excuse for parents not teaching their youngsters how to respect their weapons. The puppet didn't even fire a warning shot. But what can you do? Stop puppets from having guns? Require sissy safety locks? That makes no sense. That's just liberal scare talk, and my kindergarten students are all Republicans—or I wouldn't have them in my class."

When reached at the Las Vegas International Gun Show where the family was recovering from their loss, the father was suitably contrite. "I don't know how Bobby got out of the house without a concealed weapon. Every morning, his mother always packs a sandwich, a banana, a Bible, and heat for each of our children. It must have fallen out on the bus. All I know is that if Bobby had had that little German beauty, he would have been able to return fire and would still be with us today. I can only hope that my other children can take Bobby's memory with them and learn from his mistake. I've told all of them: 'Always get the first shot. Because the first shot can sometimes be the last.' I think the fact that it was Jesus trying to kill him might have caught him a little bit off guard. Not that I'm making excuses for him."

What Would Betty Avoid?

giving in to sin—and then detection of her failure to do so!

labels are not just for garments— inspect all of them!

As someone who (selflessly on your behalf) has paid cursory attention to how most Americans dress, I can tell you that there is an inherent problem in allowing people to choose their own labels. Regrettably, this situation is not limited to clothing. Americans give their countrymen far too much latitude when it comes to explaining why they are so annoying. People think that the antidote for obnoxious behavior is simply unearthing an exculpatory explanation—rather than stopping the offensive conduct. Therefore, it is important to learn to decipher the admissions of the perpetually self-effacing.

When someone tells you:	What they really mean is:
They have "trust issues."	They will steal your husband—or, worse, your look.
They have an "addictive personality."	Your help should be careful not to prick their fingers on heroin syringes when they clean out the wastepaper basket in the guest powder room tomorrow morning.
They have "codependency issues."	This is your last warning. Please pay close attention; this may be your only opportunity to flee.
They have "rage issues."	They manage to provoke feelings of rage in others with alarming regularity.
"I've never trusted anyone enough to tell this to before."	They are just about to say something they manage to weave into every laborious conversation simply as an excuse to keep the discussion focused on the only thing that interests them—*them.*

Never allow people to label their own psychosis. Otherwise, we would all have to refer to every busybody as "concerned" in the same way that we unblinkingly allow the appellation chosen by Concerned Women for America, which is simply a union for the Gladys Kravitzes. I know these women. They are Sisters in Christ. With hair color that replicates off-season key limes and hardwood doors, they have every reason to be concerned. But they're not concerned; they are simply meddlesome. Trust me.

So close to Jesus,
Delta lets us pool
our Skymiles.

how to spot a counterfeit christian™

It is my sad duty to inform you that Christians play the same games when it comes to labeling themselves. Truly, I can't recount the number of times I have been lied to by someone professing to be a True Christian™. Without a glimmer of conscience, people will tell me that they are True Christians™— knowing that they aren't Southern Baptist at all! Imagine such appalling disregard for the truth! I have actually been in the room when Catholics— idolatrous people whose facsimile of faith and penchant for drinking real blood hardly sets them apart from barbarous Aztecs—have spoken of "Christian faith" as if it were their own. Honestly!

To address this egregious state of affairs, I have prepared a helpful guide to assist you in recognizing Counterfeit Christians™ within two minutes of meeting them. Once you have memorized the warning signs, you will waste on Counterfeit Christians™ no more time than it takes to utter a quick, heartfelt rebuke. After all, what is the point of squandering time building a friendship in this life when it stands no chance of being continued in the next life?

Counterfeit Christian™	True Christain ™
Votes for a Demon-crat occasionally because they "like him"	Votes 100 percent God's Own Party ticket in strict conformance with the Christian Coalition's unbiased, nonpartisan Voter Guide
Episcopalian	Southern Baptist
Mealy-mouthed and cowardly, says: "Jesus didn't want us to judge"	Ready to judge for Jesus without warning or provocation
Goes to church on Sunday	Goes to church Sunday, Wednesday—and whenever the neighbors are watching
Talks to Jesus	Jesus talks to them
Knows parts of the Bible	Knows *better* parts of the Bible
Baptist	Southern Baptist
Loves the sinner, but hates the sin	Takes comfort in knowing that it is not the "sin" that will be spending eternity tortured in Hell
Thinks about homosexuals changing	Thinks about homosexuals constantly
Strives to be good and pure	Strives to be God and Puritan
Thinks Dr. Laura is obnoxious for being a hypocrite	Thinks Dr. Laura is damned for being a Jew
Thinks that Britney Spears' time is almost over and she will be going away	Thinks that Britney Spears' time is almost over and she will be going to Hell

137

WWBT?

What Would Betty Teach?

the importance of forgiveness — and then sinners a lesson

"All the News That Fits, We Print"

New York End Times

The only newspaper in America that is "Untouched by Unsaved Hands"

Heaven: low 70, high 71
Hell: 4,323°
Outlook: bleak

Creation Scientists Prove That Circles Are of Satan

FREEHOLD, IOWA (AP). The discovery that this once godly nation is full of biblically incorrect circles was made last week in connection with the firing of five members of the mathematics department at Landover Baptist University for the Saved. "Scripture at II Chronicles 4:2 tells us that Solomon made a circular metal bowl that was ten cubits in diameter and thirty cubits in circumference," recounts Dean of Creation Science Mathematics, Dr. Harold Pinto. "Now, I don't need any secular guesses that pi is equal to 3.14159265 when the Lord tells me that pi is an even 3!"

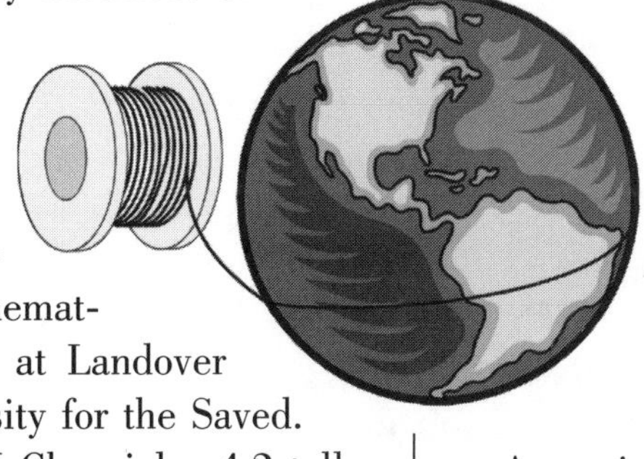

Baptist Creation scientists used rulers and a big ball of string last year to prove that the Earth is 4,000 miles wide and exactly 12,000 miles in circumference.

As scientists, the Christian researchers at Landover Baptist University for the Saved are honor bound to test and retest every scientific theory, including secular geometric principles. "We subject every scientific postulate to the most rigorous laboratory testing possible," confirmed

139

Dr. Pinto. "If a scientist comes up with a hypothesis, we open our Bible and if it is already in there, we publish a paper on it. If scripture does not support the theory, then the scientist is forbidden ever to mention it again. If he does, he is thrown out of the university and left to Satan." Using this scientifically accepted method, Landover Baptist researchers have conclusively verified that the correct value of pi is indeed exactly 3 based upon God's Word in II Chronicles 4:2.

Being True Christians™, the faculty at Landover Baptist University for the Saved takes God's Word very seriously. "We will not allow anything to contradict the inerrant word of the Lord," admonished visiting Professor of Christian Conformity Betty Bowers. After receiving her honorary M.D. (which allows her to practice Creation Medicine healings and exorcisms at Baptist hospitals throughout the land), Mrs. Bowers spoke on the issue of the heretical value for pi. "Well, I was the one who first brought it to the attention of the dean. There were several circular light fixtures in the Michael Graves lobby of the university's Olympic-size baptism pool. They caught my keen eye because of their decidedly passé 1980s cloying, postmodern touches. Upon closer inspection, I realized what was really bothering me. Their dimensions were not biblical!" Using a piece of dental floss, Mrs. Bowers discovered that the circumference of the circular glass was roughly 3.14 times the diameter of the light fixture.

"Once the Lord drew my attention to the heretical dimensions of those light fixtures, I began to realize just how much unsaved secular scientists have polluted the world around us with objects that stand in impudent rebuke of God's unerring Word. Plates, watch faces, Christian music CDs—you name it! You'd be amazed at how many things flaunt God's Word. Well that, of course, is going to change. I am having every object in my home brought in line with the Bible's infallible teaching that pi is equal to 3. I have even spoken to several companies about fixing the tires on my Bentleys. Goodyear is of the Devil and said they couldn't make the new pi = 3 tires, but I'm not going to get back in that car until it is right with the Lord! Biblical tires may affect gas mileage, but that is a small price for salvation. Praise the Lord!"

So close to Jesus,
He is delaying the Rapture
to allow my hair to grow out.

HWBV?

How Would Betty Vote?

republican—and repeatedly

Nonpartisan Christian Coalition Voter Guide

GOD'S OWN PARTY	ISSUE	DEMON-CRATS
NO	Should our tax dollars be used to rip little Christian babies from their mother's wombs and hack them to pieces in a Demon-cratic Party–sponsored Planned Parenthood butcher shop?	YES
NO	Do you support a political party that uses an ass as its symbol because that is exactly what each and every person who votes for liberal garbage is?	YES
YES	Will you throw out the liberal, namby-pamby so-called Constitution and replace it with the Holy (KJV 1611) Bible, which, because it is without error, cannot be questioned–even by our own Republican Supreme Court?	NO
NO	Will you persecute honest Christians simply for hating all the same people God hates?	YES
NO	Will you force innocent children to submit to molestation by satanic homosexual recruiters in public schools, but slap them senseless if they dare pray to the one True God?	YES

GOD'S OWN PARTY	ISSUE	DEMON-CRATS
YES	Will you agree to allow the godly Pentagon and Christian defense contractors to build trillion-dollar warheads even if our most lethal enemy has little more than catapults and vats of boiling oil?	YES
NO	Will you snatch our precious guns from our cold, dead hands until the only people who have personal assault weapons in this country are men with million-dollar rap record deals?	YES
NO	Will you cheer when babies are aborted on purpose, but arrest folks if they run over a spotted owl by accident with their minivan?	YES
NO	Will you support special rights for homosexuals, such as the so-called right to be treated like everyone else even though they are disgusting, perverted sinners who make Jesus vomit?	YES

america's best christian: spiritual adviser to america's first dysfunctional family

FROM THE LOUIS QUINZE DESK OF

Betty Bowers

AMERICA'S BEST CHRISTIAN

Dear Fellow Republicans-in-Christ:

I just returned from Camp David with the Bush family. I was called to provide spiritual solace, but the Holy Spirit was only one of many spirits that filled our teary-eyed afternoon. I was, of course, sworn to absolute secrecy. I assume, had they known about it, they would have also asked me to keep the tape recording I made of the gathering confidential, too. It is with this in mind that I ask all of you to be careful in disseminating this completely accurate transcription, as it contains rather sensitive information. I trust that you will, as have I, make it available only out of Christian concern for those frailer than yourself—and not out of any tawdry impulse to gossip.

So close to Jesus, communion tastes like leftovers,

Betty Bowers

JENNA: Okay, like, I just want to say, you know, how–

W: Dadgummit, Janna, I told you. We ain't starting this heart-to-ear stuff until 10:30.

LAURA: (Spraying Endust on linen lampshade) Now, George–

W: Woman! I am the most powerfulest man in the fried world and I said that this "familiar summit" don't get going till 10:30. Sharp.

JENNA: But, Mr. President–

W: Jeanette, I just told you! WHOA! WHOA! Yes! I am the man! I am the man! WHOA-EEE! Don't nobody say I ain't got what it takes to run the world. Look at this!

MOTHER BARBARA: George, put that Game Boy down.

W [*looking at watch*]: Okay, five, four, three, two, ONE! Blast off! It's 10:30. We can start this little family get-together stuff.

LAURA: Okay, girls, your father wants a word with you. Jenna, you sit over there. And–ah, um you in the chartreuse-like tank toppy thing, sit on the other side of your sister.

DAUGHTER BARBARA: This isn't chartreuse.

LAURA: It certainly looks red.

BETTY: Laura, chartreuse is green, dear. Though not quite that bilious shade you're wearing.

LAURA: Don't you think Scaasi is divine, Betty? He did all of George's mother's clothes when she was in the White House.

BETTY: Well, at least we know he's used to overcoming large obstacles–

MOTHER BARBARA: Watch it, Betty!

POPPY: Enough of this girly talk.

W: I don't mind girly talk.

MOTHER BARBARA: What a shocker! Get a load of Mr. Cheerleader everyone!

POPPY: Don't start in on that again, Bar.

W: Well, I have got me a girl I need to talk to right now.

DAUGHTER BARBARA: Mr. President, there are two of us.

LAURA: Jenna, make room for, um, ur, the one not wearing chartreuse.

DAUGHTER BARBARA: *Barbara.*

LAURA: I knew that. Don't smart-mouth me, Miss Harvard.

DAUGHTER BARBARA: *Yale.*

LAURA: If you say so. Anyway, sit closer, so your father remembers you're here.

W: I guess you know what I want to talk about. Did you see that little seven-year-old catch that fly ball at T-ball? Dang it! Well I'll be dipped in hawg shi–

MOTHER BARBARA: George! Get to the point.

W: You mean about these two drunks?

JENNA: Ain't neither!

W: Yartoo!

JENNA: Ain't neither!

W: Yartoo!

JENNA: Ain't neither!

W: Yartoo!

MOTHER BARBARA: Stop it, you two!

W: I'm the most influenced man in the whole dang world. I don't take sass. In all my born days, I ain't never—

MOTHER BARBARA: Knock off that stupid barnyard Texas talk, George. While America will accept even the most patrician dynasty as one of them, as long as you pronounce it "Amur-ka," there's no press in here. We're rich. Talk like it for God's sake.

W: Sorry, Mommy.

BETTY: Yes, I think it safe to say that whichever Pope originated the expression "money talks" didn't have something out of Steinbeck in mind. Anyway, let's shift the emphasis here a bit. Jenna and Barbara—

MOTHER BARBARA: What?

BETTY: I meant the one who doesn't look like a gargoyle, dear. Now, girls, there is nothing particularly wrong with drinking. After all, as True Christians™ we have told our nation's children to ask themselves "What would Jesus do?" before making any decision. And if you will recall, Jesus is someone who squandered His very first miracle on getting liquor for his boozehound of a mother—

LAURA: Jenna, freshen this, sweetie. Not so much icey-icey.

BETTY: As I was saying, Jesus appeared to be at the beck and call of a mother who had an appalling habit of braying for free Chablis the second the bar ran dry—

LAURA: And don't put too much coconut milk in it. No point in filling a tumbler with a mixer—the ice melts anyway. Ice: Nature's time-released little mixer!

MOTHER BARBARA: Oh, put a sock in it, Laura. Betty's talking.

POPPY: And at about $3,000 a sentence.

BETTY: If you wanted spiritual advice on the cheap, you should have called Jesse Jackson. You could have had him for cab fare. Anyway, what I was telling these dear, fragile Christian girls is that since Jesus was wont to turn tap water into an alcoholic beverage, one should never ask, "What would Jesus do?" within ten feet of a liquor bottle without a designated atheist.

LAURA: That's why we gave them the Secret Service.

BETTY: Would that the girls could keep their *bar* service secret.

So close to Jesus, we can't stand all the same people.

MOTHER BARBARA: Amen!

BETTY: Let us open our Bibles.

LAURA: I seem to have misplaced mine. Oh, here it is.

BETTY: Laura, that is the Lord's Word. Not a coaster. Turn to Matthew, chapter 11. George, I think Matthew is designated with a purple walrus in your book.

POPPY: Matthew. Wasn't that the guy there who was that tax collector fellow?

W: A "tax and spend" Democrat! We ought to be reading a Gospel by a guy who wanted to give money *away*!

BETTY: That would be Jesus, dear.

W: Darn straight. A Republican.

POPPY: But didn't that Jesus guy want us to give *our* money away?

MOTHER BARBARA: Smacks of socialism, if you ask me! He better not sing that tune in Kennebunkport.

BETTY: How many times do I have to tell you? With skilled biblical interpretation, you can effortlessly follow even the more inconvenient passages. When Jesus said, "Give away everything you have to the poor," He was talking to people who had nothing to give. So, I try to follow their example and also give nothing to the so-called poor.

W: Sounds pretty Republican to me!

BETTY: Exactly. Anyway, I'd like to read from Matthew 11:19. "The Son of man came eating and drinking, and they say, Behold a man gluttonous, and a winebibber, a friend of publicans—"

MOTHER BARBARA: Betty, my Bible says, "friend of *Republicans*."

BETTY: You must have Friend-of-Our-Lord Pat Robertson's Bible, dear. He's been looking for it.

W: What is a windbibber? Someone who farts? [*giggles*]

BETTY: A *winebibber*. A drunkard. Surely, that word isn't foreign to you, dear. Anyway, do you see, girls, what Our Lord's inerrant Word is saying?

JENNA: That, like, Jesus was a partier?

DAUGHTER BARBARA: Cool. Jesus was a drunk, too.

BETTY: Well, not exactly—

MOTHER BARBARA: See how Christlike your father has been all these years? You didn't grow up with a lot of mushy talk and touching, but we did give you girls Christian values.

LAURA: Jenna, stop chewing your hair.

MOTHER BARBARA: Barbara, fix Grandma another bloody M. And not so much celery salt in it this time. You know I'm on a low-sodium health diet. Are you trying to kill me?

POPPY: Well, girls, you know we love you—

MOTHER BARBARA: What your grandfather is trying to say is, we are furious with you two. We've been very lenient. Even though your father talks like his job requires him to go where the vegetables are ripe, thanks to our family name, he has millions squirreled away for you girls. Your parents have given you everything—

LAURA: Except our time. Parents are entitled to something they can call their own. I'm a teacher—

MOTHER BARBARA: Laura, I'll handle this. Like I said, you've been given everything. And we only asked for one thing in return!

JENNA: Not to be drunks like you all?

MOTHER BARBARA: No! Not to get caught, you idiot!

W: Well, it's not their fault. It's the liberal media. It just isn't fair to report when they get arrested. Hell's bells, I don't even report the times I get arrested, I don't know why them liberal reporters got to stick their noses in private family matters.

POPPY: George, they got citations. It's a matter of public record.

LAURA: Well, it never would have been public if they had just watched us a little closer! Honestly, girls. I've told you a million times. "Beer after liquor, never sicker—booze before press, what a mess!"

What Would Betty Pack?

three outfits a day—and then some heat!

what every saved woman should have in her purse in case of rapture

A PRADA LABEL. I would never entertain the sensation of envy because it is a sin, and, let's be honest for a moment, an event or person who would inspire such a coarse feeling in me is statistically improbable. Nevertheless, I am not averse to provoking such an unattractive emotion in others (indeed, every time I leave one of my lovely homes I am reminded of my inability to do otherwise). Consider the unchecked envy provoked by a Prada bag here on Earth. Now, imagine the delicious reaction one can expect in Heaven where there are no stores.

A KJV BIBLE. I unflinchingly adhere to the belief that when promises are involved, it is always good to have them in writing. In case God were to try to go back on His Word (particularly the bit about there being riches and mansions in Heaven), it would be very convenient to have something neatly highlighted with which to confront Him. If He waffles, remind Him about the bit that the Bible is "inerrant" and "timeless."

A QUALITY MOISTURIZER. Ascension into Heaven will require more, not less, vigilance in adhering to a well-crafted skin-care regime. Anyone who has spent as much time in a Gulfstream jet as I have can attest to the drying effects of high altitudes. Besides, if you don't like your skin at forty, imagine how disappointed with its elasticity you will be at one million and forty.

DIAMONDS. Keep in mind, Heaven will be a barter economy and diamonds will be readily exchanged for accommodations with a view of one of the more ostentatious galaxies. Take a lovely diamond bracelet, and pop out the stones that you need, depending on the surmised desperation of the seraphim you are dealing with.

A PAIR OF QUALITY OPAQUE UNDERWEAR. In picking a suitable wardrobe for Heaven, one must be mindful of the unique circumstance of being a weightless apparition. Yes, you can finally squeeze into something a full two sizes smaller, but do so in the knowledge that people will be constantly flying beneath you. This is just one reason why harlots who eschew undergarments are not welcome in Heaven.

A POCKET SPRAY FRAGRANCE. Remember a lot of the people in Heaven have no sense of personal hygiene or died wearing something they had been in for several months. This is usually because they either lived in a century before indoor plumbing or are from France. You will find it helpful to spritz your most pungent fragrance with regularity and the precision of a crop duster.

A PACKET OF QUALITY BREATH MINTS. People who have been dead several centuries cannot be relied upon for the freshest breath. Most, of course, you will wish to eschew conversation with entirely, but for those who capture your attention, a lovely prelude to any tête-à-tête is, "Care for a mint, dear?" If the answer is no, feign some urgent matter with the Lord.

A PAIR OF BLACK GUCCI SUNGLASSES. They saved Jackie from looking at O—and they will save you from being caught looking bored by the Almighty. You will find that the substratospheric glare is almost as unbearable as listening to Mary go on and on about all the "cool ideas" she had that were attributed to her offspring in the Bible. Wearing perfectly opaque lenses, you will be able to keep an eye on others (to spot any damnable mischief), while pretending to listen to each of the many thousands of words Mary will utter. As soon as you see someone doing something they shouldn't, you can then excuse yourself from Mary's self-absorbed drone by saying, "I must turn someone in to God." (Make sure you say this with pitch-perfect elocution, pausing to separate "in" and "to." Being a woman Catholics have wildly promoted, Mary gets very territorial if she thinks you've just said you are going to "turn someone *into* God.")

A SMALL LOADED HANDGUN. God would not have called upon us to join the NRA if He didn't expect us to employ the skills we are taught on Earth in Heaven. In fact, it is rather irresponsible to make yourself beautiful when you don't learn how to maim men who will inevitably make unwelcome advances. When I am sporting a new outfit that displays my fabulous legs, I often find occasion to disable a gawking stranger with a well-placed warning shot to their foot. I have the barrel of my semiautomatic coyly peeking out of the end of my Prada clutch. If a man I don't know brandishes a lascivious leer, I simply look as if I am going for a breath mint and he never even sees it coming. Such weapons, of course, lose their efficacy when directed at spirits in the Hereafter, but you will find that people recoil at the sound of gunfire, if only from instinct, which will achieve the desired goal.

So close to Jesus,

the hotel manager smirks
when I check in "alone."

A PALM PILOT. You are going to meet a lot of people in Heaven. (Figure, conservatively: 20 per day = 140 per week = 7,280 per year = 72,800 per decade = 7,280,000,000 per million years.) So it will be difficult to keep track mentally of which ones you can trust and to whom you told your real age to or loaned money.

BOTOX INJECTIONS. The phrase "I swear you look ten years younger!" begins to lose its potency when you are well into your fourth millennium, dear.

MACE. People who would know better than to approach you on Earth will think they can talk to you simply because you both happen to be in Heaven. Be prepared for this annoying misapprehension.

WWBD?

What Will Betty Do?

how to succeed at the expense of others in the afterlife

When you have the rapt attention of the Almighty as often as I do, you learn to listen with nuanced attention. At first, simply due to the novelty of conversing with someone so famous, I listened to each declamatory utterance. I even embarrassed myself by feeling the need to respond to every rhetorical question. (I found that the Lord does not like to be interrupted—or corrected.) Over time, I learned when to pay close attention and when to nod with feigned assent while mentally redecorating my Villa Cristo de Amalfi in Ravello. (It turned out beautifully.)

I often find the Lord's asides and ripostes, usually uttered late in the evening or when someone dreadful has just left the planet, are some of His most illuminating comments. The Lord's spontaneity might surprise some who naively assume the omniscient are incapable of the unplanned. Nevertheless, since God decided to give humans "free will," He has been nothing but surprised by the unseemly and (His Word) stupid way people have used this license to veer from divine sensibilities. Of course, being all-knowing, He is aware that He is going to be shocked ahead of time, which somewhat undercuts the surprise. Nevertheless, it is most often the Lord's wry observations in response to human folly that have provided me with the clearest insights into not only the surest way to get into Heaven, but also how best to succeed and flourish upon arrival.

Fortunately for my readers, when it comes to issues of self-preservation, whether it is good skin care or even salvation, I have learned to pay careful attention—and keep notes. Now that we are near the end of this book, it comes time to disabuse you of some precious notions.

SURVIVALTIP Heaven is a lot like Las Vegas—novel as an idea, but, frankly, a little cheesy in the execution. After ten minutes trying to drive with the blinding glare from a street paved with gold, you will be longing for a place with roads paved less ostentatiously with merely good intentions.

The biggest misconception about Heaven is that everyone is going to be blandly pleasant. I don't know where this outrageous idea came from. In any event, it is important to remember who is going to Heaven: humans, not strenuously polite automatons or Jehovah's Witnesses. To think that humans after five minutes, much less one billion years, are not going to lapse into petty one-upmanship and impatient barbs is quixotic at best. After all, contrary to popular belief, Heaven is a place of politics, alliances, fights, and grudges. If you don't think so, then how was Lucifer able to recruit battalions of disgruntled (and probably unionized) seraphim to jostle for better working conditions?

betty's exclusive interview with the blessed virgin

The following is a transcript of an interview Mrs. Bowers conducted on her television program *The Bowers Hour* during sweeps.

BETTY: First of all, I want to thank you for taking time out of your day to meet with me.

THE BVM: Time is one thing I've got plenty of.

BETTY: You know, that is the one aspect of Heaven I've never been too keen on. People in Heaven go on *forever*. Like a Kevin Costner movie. I find the prospect of a social eternity daunting since most humans run out of things to say before dessert or forty. After that, it's just like summer on ABC. Reruns and deceptive self-promotion.

THE BVM: I know. I'm just glad I wasn't on Earth when people like Methuselah were living to be almost a thousand.

BETTY: I can't even imagine thirty without Retinol!

THE BVM: Everyone was living way too long back then. Even God realized that mistake. So He killed them off in the flood. Not because they were extraordinarily sinful, but just because He couldn't take one more minute of hearing the same prayers for new hips for the millionth time.

BETTY: And it can't be much better in Heaven where you have an infinite number of days before you—surrounded by people who are telling the same story for the 789,435th time.

THE BVM: Exactly! And what was funny three hundred years ago is only funny after wine.

BETTY: And I would imagine what was funny a thousand years ago is never funny.

THE BVM: Especially if they are Germanic. All those people we let into Heaven from, say, 450 to about 1600—and there weren't many—have a very crude, scatological sense of humor that nobody finds at all entertaining—outside of black sitcom audiences. People don't think about that. All the inhabitants of Heaven grew up in different eras and cultures. Once the euphoria of "I'm not being tortured in Hell" wears off, most people find that they don't really like those from other countries or epochs.

what will betty do?

BETTY: Well, I can barely tolerate a moment with my own contemporaries. I have no intention of exerting all this effort to get into Heaven, only to squander my reward in the company of filthy foreign people who lived before Prozac. No offense.

THE BVM: None taken. I think. We have folks from dull times in history, but the good thing is that we don't have anyone who died in that really squalid B.C. period.

BETTY: Praise the Lord! Who wants to be in the company of people who lived before the era of quality jewelry?

THE BVM: Well, actually, it is because they lived before Jesus saved humanity, so they were sent to Hell.

BETTY: That, too. Salvation is just like anything: it all comes down to timing. So, given the obvious dearth of well-crafted conversation, what do you do to occupy your time, dear?

THE BVM: Are you kidding me? I need a staff of seraphim just to keep up with my personal-appearance junkets. I'll tell you, if it were up to me, I'd stay home. When I took the job—you know, at the Annunciation—I was told "one week of travel a month *max.*" You know, but they always tell you that to get you to take the job and then they change it.

So close to Jesus,
I'm the one who tells Him
He has pesto in His teeth.

BETTY: Well, in fairness to God, I am sure He had no idea what the Catholics were going to do with you. They turned an incubator into a goddess. No offense, but even Jesus didn't have a lot of time for you in the Bible, dear.

THE BVM: We've processed that. The sting from "What do I want with you, woman?" is only slightly less painful now—two thousand years later. No mother should have a son who talks to her like that. But you try disciplining God! You wonder why I stayed in the background so much.

BETTY: Well, you've certainly made up for it since. No wonder Jesus and the Holy Spirit call you Eve Harrington behind your back.

THE BVM: It's not my fault I'm popular. I'm not just kvetching here, but last month I had three weeks in Latin America. And those people don't honor personal space.

BETTY: It is an axiom of humanity: Respect for personal space is inversely proportional to the amount of deodorant applied. Your popularity is so odd to me because you are hardly even mentioned in the Bible, but since the Middle Ages you've been popping up on every taco shell and windshield from Sicily to Tijuana. I've always found this to be odd since, apart from failing to be proactive enough to book a hotel room, your most famous biblical contribution was pestering your son for more wine.

THE BVM: Ah, the wedding in Cana. What a disaster. You've read about the caterer, but you should have seen the flowers. The only thing that saved the whole thing was me nagging Jesus.

BETTY: Honestly, dear, you acted like some deplorable boozehound. A Christian lady knows that when she has drunk all the liquor in sight, it is probably a good time to stop drinking, not complain in a braying voice that the liquor has run out. The truly reverent beseech the Almighty for salvation, not free booze. I'm sure it was rather embarrassing for Him and the hostess that you were making such a frantic scene. Such antics today would land you in Betty Ford. And to waste a perfectly good miracle. Jesus could have brought someone back from the dead. But—no—you had to have another glass of chablis!

THE BVM: The bride's parents never complained.

BETTY: Anyway, I have a few questions for you, dear.

THE BVM: Before we get into that, can we get something out of the way? I didn't appreciate that crack you made about me on September 27, 1994, about the "tartish unmarried teenagers having sex with the King of Kings."

BETTY: I'm almost certain I was referring to Priscilla Presley, dear.

THE BVM: Maybe I'm projecting. Whatever. Okay, fire away.

BETTY: Is there anything about religion in America that you would like to see changed?

THE BVM: How much time do you have? [*Laughs*] Let me see. Well, basically three things. First, less attention on the Holy Ghost. [*Yawns and looks at her watch*] Second, more attention on me!

BETTY: So, in other words, we should all become hellbound Catholics. Oh, that was fabulous!

THE BVM: What was?

BETTY: When you said "me," this wonderfully warm light bathed the entire room.

THE BVM: Well, it's like I always say: There's not a woman in this universe who can't benefit from radiant backlighting. How did it play on the fabric?

BETTY: Completely ethereal.

THE BVM: Perfect! Apparitions so often overlook the importance of good production values. So where was I? Oh, I know. And the third thing people need to do is get back to animal sacrifices.

BETTY: Animal sacrifices? Say it isn't so.

THE BVM: Oh, please. Humans will mow children down in junior high school with semi-automatic weapons, starve half an African village to death, but they won't put mascara on a rabbit? My Husband is just so not getting that.

BETTY: You talk about "my husband." To whom are you referring?

THE BVM: To whom do you think I'm referring? Do you think I have multiple spouses? I mean, hel-LO? We don't live in Utah!

BETTY: Well, if you did, I wouldn't be wasting my time speaking to you. Besides, they allow only the men to have multiple spouses in Utah.

THE BVM: That is just so typical of this planet. Don't get me started on human men. But what would you expect from some Johnny-come-lately religion without a strong mother-worshiping tradition, anyway?

BETTY: Well, one does have to admire the Mormons for the resourceful synergy of hallucinatory imagination and boundless gullibility. It makes for the most amusingly far-fetched tenets outside of Reaganomics. But getting back to your connubial status, I thought you were married to Joseph, dear.

THE BVM: Annulled. It was never consummated. Not for lack of trying.

BETTY: Pity you aren't a Kennedy. Their trying is always successful, and they still manage to get annulments at very reasonable prices. So you are saying you married God?

THE BVM: Well, if you are going to be a trophy wife, you could do worse.

BETTY: But are you and God actually married?

THE BVM: Look, I had His Kid. You'd think I'd have gotten a ring out of it. Right? But no. He's very cagey. He keeps saying, "How can we be married before God, when I am God?" It's so annoying when He gets obtuse like that; He thinks He's being clever. *Not.*

BETTY: So sad that even a male who could create a perfect wife still can't find someone He'd commit to. Why is He so reluctant?

THE BVM: I think He's really worried. You know, if we divorced, I'd get half of everything. Literally. And that's a lot. Besides, we'd argue over who got Earth. But I'd probably end up being the one stuck with it.

BETTY: Would our little planet be so bad, dear?

THE BVM: Well, as planets go, it is pretty nice looking. I particularly like some of the Four Seasons resort properties. But, I've got to tell you, out of all the trillions of planets, there are only two of them where the inhabitants wear blended fabrics or pretend to speak for God. Earth was not the first, as usual. [*Laughs*] But it does it the most. As you can imagine, that doesn't exactly sit well with Him. I mean, He used to get mad at me. Like when reports of that dyke Joan of Arc filtered back to Him. I wasn't even involved in that, but He thought I had sent Saint Michael down to talk on His behalf. *As if.* I don't even know this Joan person—besides, I was on vacation that century. No offense, but that whole Middle Ages was so dull! Like the 1980s. But it really hit the fan that week.

BETTY: You don't know Joan of Arc?

THE BVM: I don't know any of those French women who say they know me! Name-droppers! Like that mousy Bernadette woman. Like I'm going to loiter in some nasty, clammy grotto waiting for some delusional, drab bore to talk at me in French! You know, not even polite enough to ask if I speak the language! Which I don't. So typically arrogant! I mean, hel-LO?? I can say "merci"—not that a deity ever would, of course.

BETTY: You don't understand French?

THE BVM: Does anyone understand the French? [*Laughing*] No, seriously, The Bird speaks it beautifully—especially after a bowl of wine, but, that's His specialty—tongues. But I can't keep up with all the human languages. There are just too many of them. I mean, I buy the tapes, I buy the CD-ROMs, but who has the time? Years ago, I took time away from poker to learn Esperanto. Never again. Basically, if it isn't Arabic, Latin, some Mandarin, or English, no can do.

BETTY: So, if someone prays in Polish, you won't understand?

THE BVM: Not a word. Which, incidentally, didn't exactly help them out in the 1930s.

BETTY: Even if a Pope prays in Polish?

THE BVM: A what?

Biblical Shopping Tip:
Are you unable to put together a saucy, yet chaste Judgment Day outfit with that "Pick me, Lord!" quality that may mean the difference between being called to God's Glory and being consigned to the Hereafter with waterfront property on a Lake of Fire? Take time now to pull together a delightful Judgment Day look. Remember: Judgment Day first impressions last an eternity.

159

BETTY: The Pope.

THE BVM: You've lost me.

BETTY: The Pope. In Rome.

THE BVM: Oh, that guy! I know whom you're talking about. I love his hats! They are beyond fabulous. Not everyone can pull off that kind of height. I'd try it, but we can't get that kind of workmanship in Heaven. So, Popes have prayed in Polish? Who knew? Oh, it really doesn't matter. We always know what it's all about anyway. Everybody always wants something. Besides, with the Internet, we're going "all English" this year.

BETTY: God uses the Internet?

THE BVM: Not for important stuff, like damning people or asking them to kill their children—the connection speeds are still too slow, but we all use AOL to meet people. Funny story: God likes to go into the Christian chat room on AOL, and tell people He is God. You should hear the cocks crowing! They always deny Him. Some woman called SavedChristian called him a "filthy liar!" and got an AOL Chat Room Guide to boot Him off for "room disruption"! In the scheme of things, not a real smart move.

BETTY: What happened to SavedChristian?

THE BVM: She was downloaded. [*Laughs*] He cracks me up when He says that! Downloaded. I love that! But she won't be lonely; most of those screen names on AOL are going to Hell. In fact, Hell is an awful lot like AOL—without all those annoying, slow-loading graphics. Mind if I smoke?

BETTY: Well, actually, yes. I do.

THE BVM: Okay. Well, let me ask it to you this way: Mind if I don't have one of my seraphim minions smite you while I smoke? [*Lighting up*] I read what you wrote about that thing my Son said about a camel passing through the eye of a needle. He stopped smoking about six hundred years ago, so he didn't find the cigarette joke funny. You know what those reformed smokers are like—holier than thou.

BETTY: I don't recall what I said.

THE BVM: You said the "passing a camel through the eye of a needle" scripture was just a warning against smoking unfiltered cigarettes while altering a hem.

BETTY: Well, to read it any other way would seem to indicate that Jesus didn't want me to have a beach home. No American is going to pay attention to a book that makes them feel guilty for buying lovely things.

THE BVM: Which is why we have only a few Americans in Heaven. Can't say we didn't warn you.

BETTY: You must be mistaken. America is God's country.

THE BVM: God doesn't make celebrity endorsements. I do. But no one asks.

BETTY: I refuse to believe that I won't be surrounded by Americans in the Afterlife!

THE BVM: You will.

BETTY: My readers are very curious about Heaven.

THE BVM: Oh, change of subject. Heaven can be summed up in one word: obnoxious.

BETTY: I think you are mistaken, dear.

THE BVM: No, I don't think I am mistaken, *dear*—since of the two of us I'm the only one who has actually been there. I mean, the place is full of really awful people. We have whole clouds full of murderers and hookers. Horrible, crude people who luckily remembered to accept Jesus Christ as their Personal Savior moments before dying—and voilà! They are in Heaven. It's crazy, but those are the rules.

BETTY: But it's not just enough to accept Jesus. You also have to love your neighbor.

THE BVM: And you're America's Best Christian? Read your Bible. You don't have to *love* your neighbor. You don't even have to be nice to them. You only have to love *Jesus* with all your heart. I guess you can tell who writes this stuff. [*Laughs*] You only have to treat your neighbor as you would treat yourself. See the difference? The Golden Rule can lead to wild results with the grossly dysfunctional. Frankly, we get a lot of masochists with Tourette's syndrome. The salt of the Earth.

BETTY: And the saltiest of the Earth's language. Oh, dear. I suppose you end up with a lot of entertainers then.

THE BVM: None of the decent ones. We've got the Singing Nun and that one fucking song she sings. Tell me that doesn't get mind-numbing!

BETTY: You mentioned "the bird" earlier. Who is that?

THE BVM: Oh, don't get me started. [*Laughs*] That's what I call the Holy Ghost. "TB" for short.

161

BETTY: Is there a problem between you and the Holy Ghost?

THE BVM: TB just likes to be the center of attention. He's behind this whole Charismatic Movement taking over My-Son-ianity, where people are obsessed with The Bird. I mean, even the name was His idea! Charismatic! Isn't that a my-Husband-damned joke? I said, "Word, Bird: The last thing any of those hill-billies gurgling saliva and rolling around in hysterical convulsions have is charisma!"

BETTY: Well, you certainly have a point there. How long has this feud been going on?

THE BVM: It seems like eternity, but it's probably a few years short of that. The Bird has serious self-esteem issues—you try being just a third of a person—and is always getting in a snit about something. For example, we were at some black-wing function and I was talking to Marie Antoinette, who's a riot; she cracks me up—

BETTY: Marie Antoinette is in Heaven?

THE BVM: Most of her. We don't get into human class squabbles—too difficult to keep up with. Especially with the French; they are always mad at someone. Anyway, we were laughing over the "Let them eat cake" comment—which, you know, she never said, but it's funny anyway—and The Bird was trying to get her atten-tion, which was getting real annoying. So, I said, very politely, "Word, Bird: You fly through my halo one more time while I'm trying to talk, there are going to be some seriously singed feathers and the Trinity is going to be the Duality *pronto.*"

BETTY: And did He stop?

THE BVM: He did something really disgusting in my hair. And we don't have running water in Heaven, so that is a real problem.

BETTY: So, this feud between you and the Holy Spirit started at this cocktail party?

THE BVM: No, it goes back way before that! TB's still got his feathers ruffled over all that Marian worship during the Middle Ages. I know He was behind the advent of Protestantism—just to keep me in my place. I can't prove it, but it has TB writ-ten all over it.

BETTY: I'm a bit surprised such unseemly politics go on in Heaven.

THE BVM: I admit; it can get sort of petty. About seven hundred years ago—no, maybe not that long—anyway, we were all at this public-appearance thing. The open-ing of a mall or something. Anyway, I was busy talking with Jesus, you know, and I didn't realize that I had stepped in front of The Bird, which is a big no-no!

So, anyway, instead of just tapping me on the shoulder with his beak, He has to make a fuss and thunder in front of everyone, "Get thee behind me, Mary!"

BETTY: I always thought that expression was first uttered by Diana Ross.

THE BVM: Another one of my favorite singers I'm never going to get to see! No, that "get thee behind me" business was just The Bird pulling rank, as usual. (Rolls eyes) You see, supernal protocol says that when it comes to folks who can stand in front of me, there are only three. Though, technically, they're regarded as one person. It's very confusing. Especially when you're trying to fill out a dinner table. And you go: "Boy, girl, boy, girl, boy, girl, *bird*."

BETTY: But I thought there was no sex in Heaven.

THE BVM: Unless you know how to work it. [*Laughs*]

BETTY: Please don't be vulgar. I meant gender, dear. But "The Bird," as you say, is the completion of the Trinity.

THE BVM: Your word. You ask me—and no one does—that's just something humans made up. But TB, of course, latched on to it because it places him closer to the action. And don't think you all down here are the only ones who debate that Trinity business! We argue about that one all the time—especially when we're ordering Chinese. Lord, Jesus, and The Bird are definitely three people when they're eating, but when it comes time to split the bill, then it's a different story! I always get stuck paying half, which is why I end up having to do more of these personal-appearance gigs than they do! I tell you, girls: It is a man's Afterworld!

Oh, my Husband! Look at the time. My Son, in about twenty minutes I need to be in some country that I've never even heard of—a little scheduling snafu. One of my seraphim staff has this crazy attitude that once she got to Heaven her work was over. Who tells people these things? I'd fire her, but she's about the only Caucasian we got up there, so what can you do?

How Would Betty Conclude?

from the diary of america's best christian: *quality time with your personal savior*

11:07 P.M., Bowers' manse, Atlanta

As is almost always the case, by the time I arrived home, Mr. Bowers and my children were in bed. I had Maria bring me a lovely glass of Brunello. When I walked into my private dressing room, I found Jesus lying back on the sofa, flipping through an article by Dominick Dunne in *Vanity Fair.* "You bet he killed her," Jesus muttered in disgust as He closed the magazine. I asked Him what He had been reading, and He joked that I could comfort myself by knowing that He had created at least one name-dropper more shameless than I. I took this as quite an uncalled-for affront, as I think there is a rather enormous difference between Dominick recounting a lunch with Joey Heatherton and my regaling someone with the de-

So close to Jesus,

people in line in front of me at the bank are instantly struck dead when I am in a rush.

tails of a charming supper with Jesus. After all, I told Jesus, "When it comes to parlaying your name into literary notoriety, I'm doing nothing Matthew, Mark, Luke, and John didn't do before me, so don't change the rules on me now." Anyway, when faced with so-called constructive criticism, I always like to return the favor. I didn't think it was appropriate for a male to walk into a Christian woman's boudoir (unless it is the spouse, and only then when specifically invited), but I didn't have the energy to chide Jesus, so I quite graciously allowed the breach to pass without comment. That is just the type of forgiving Christian that I am. (Besides, there is a rather delightful economy in conversation when the other person can read your mind.)

Apparently, Jesus did know that I had seen Him this morning before the elevator doors were actually closing. He seemed vaguely annoyed that I thought that I had outsmarted Him. I tried to cover as best I could. I told Him that since He is always on my mind, I see Him all the time anyway, so I am never sure if it is really Him or just my wistful imagining. It sounded like a load of nonsense to me, but it seemed to mollify Him. I also reminded Him that it is a lot easier for Him to get around. Not being an apparition, I need to be driven, so I couldn't always linger to chat. I think what hurt Him the most was that He thought I was fleeing His company to see Jerry Falwell at the Bringing Integrity To Christian Homemakers awards breakfast. When He finally articulated this, we both burst out laughing at the spectacle of anyone fleeing *toward* Jerry.

After He had a glass of Brunello, bygones were bygones, and I was prepared to end the evening in the lovely way that most of my days conclude. It is my favorite part of the day, sipping an unpretentious wine while having a tête-à-tête with my Personal Savior. Honestly, it is such a novelty not to have to talk down to someone. True, it limits my skillful abilities to embellish when I know He has actually been watching. Further, it is a challenge to be amusing when the person with whom you are speaking already knows everything you are going to say. Nevertheless, these slight inconveniences attendant to speaking with the omniscient are more than compensated for by the deliciously gossipy things that Someone who knows everything can add to a lull in any conversation.

BTCG

Betty's True Christian™ Glossary

ACTIVIST—Anyone you disagree with. Thus, "activist" judges, "activist" unions, "activist" school boards, and "activist" homosexuals.

AGENDA—All political objectives you oppose. Demon-crats, lie-berals, feminists, homosexuals, and environmentalists have "agendas." True Christian™ political groups have "hopes," "callings," "dreams," "bullets of righteousness," and "godly plans of action."

BOYCOTT—God's preferred method of social change unless you are black. If the targeted organization capitulates to a boycott, it is proof of "the power of God to change hearts." However, if a boycott is unsuccessful, it proves the organization being boycotted is "hardened," "in the grip of the Devil," and on a one-way trip straight to Hell, despite your selfless efforts.

BROKEN FAMILIES—Refers only to the divorces of other people (but not any of your own). Families are never "broken" or "shattered" by bad marriages, domestic violence, child abuse, incest, or molestation.

CAREER—Something a man, as God-ordained head of the house, has. Careers for women are "destructive," "selfish," and "unfulfilling" compared to full-time child rearing and home schooling, where women who were not able to complete the ninth grade are called by God to prepare their children for college. Women who attempt to balance family and career are "shirking their God-given responsibility" and are responsible for creating another "generation without values." Note: "Career" does not include multimillion-dollar Christian television ministries, working for Concerned Women for America, or having your own syndicated call-in advice show.

CHILD MOLESTATION–Something wicked homosexuals do to our innocent children. It is claimed to occur much more frequently in the family, but this can't be true as polite people would never even talk about such.

CHRISTIAN COALITION–*See* Love Offering, Republican.

CIVIL RIGHTS–The concept of equal legal rights applies to everyone. The exception is Homosexual Americans. (*See* Special Rights.)

COMPASSION–An emotion spoken of in public and saved for disgusting people who are going straight to Hell.

DEATH PENALTY–A form of punishment not used often enough. Most True Christians™ long for the day when this is implemented against unrepentant homosexuals and lesbians. (*See* Compassion.) The only time the death penalty is not considered "God's mighty judgment" is when a death row inmate has become a born-again Christian. Then, the death penalty is "unnecessary" and seen as an "impediment to further ministry" by the inmate slated for execution.

DECEPTION–Term describing the state of being a fellow Christian is in if they disagree with you on a social or theological issue. For example, if another Christian holds views that are pro-choice, pro-homosexual rights, or antideath penalty, then they are "deceived." If the same Christian makes a logical, reasoned argument for their position, then they are "misled." If the same Christian also makes a scriptural argument for their position, then they are "false teachers," "rebellious," and guilty of "twisting the Word." (*See* Liberal.)

DISNEY–The main force behind the Collapse of Traditional Moral Values, and one of society's greatest threats to the Family. Creation Scientists have proven that Disney is responsible for over 70 percent of subliminal homosexual recruitment pornography seen by our innocent children.

DOMESTIC PARTNER BENEFITS–Given by most amoral businesses to encourage sin. A sign of "collapsing moral values" and the impending Apocalypse.

DOMESTIC VIOLENCE–A mythical problem that does not affect the family, does not injure or kill Christian women, and is never to be addressed by polite people.

FAMILY–Unit of: heterosexual male head of household married for life to heterosexual female homemaker, with biological home-schooled children conceived without birth control or pleasure and born at least nine months after marriage. All members of the family must be members of a conservative Bible-based church or they are not Family. (*See* Sinners.)

FEMINISTS–Women who are not sufficiently submissive. Responsible for: neglected children, teenage pregnancy, unemployed males, poor SAT scores, breakdown of the Family. (*See* Gay/Lesbian.)

GAY CHRISTIANS–Something that does not exist. Those who claim this title are "trapped" in a state of Deception, and are first in line for the Lake of Fire because they "twist God's Word." To save them, True Christians™ must exercise Compassion and tell them that God would rather see them dead than loved.

GAY/LESBIAN–Homosexual is the preferred term, as it focuses more explicitly on sex. With feminists and liberals, responsible for nearly all social ills (with the possible exception of abortion). (*See* Jews.)

GOD–*See* Republican.

GUNS–The love of which separates True Christians™ from godless Liberals. A bullet from a gun doesn't kill (the person pulling the trigger does), so guns should not be banned. A drug from a syringe, however, does get you high (not the person pushing the plunger) and should be banned. If you don't understand this distinction, you are not a True Christian™ or a Real American.

HATE CRIMES–Something made up by the Militant Radical Homosexual Agenda to limit our ability to openly hate people God–quite coincidentally–also hates.

HETEROSEXUALS–Never used. Assumed to be everyone on Earth, except for tiny number of "Militant Radical Homosexual Activists."

HOLLYWOOD–The source of all evil in Western Civilization. Controlled by Disney, Jews, feminists, liberals, and "Militant Radical Homosexual Activists," or AOL–Time Warner when a new rap album is released. Also known as "Mystery Babylon" and "the pit of Hell."

HOMOSEXUALS–Tiny minority of "Militant Radical Activists" seeking Special Rights, hiring quotas, and the destruction of the Family. Recent phenomenon that did not exist before secular television, signaling that the End Is Near.

JEWS–God's chosen people who are going straight to Hell.

JUDICIAL SYSTEM–Varying definitions. When ruling against you, it is "activist judges" subverting the "will of the people." Otherwise, a perfectly acceptable way of enforcing God's Will.

LADIES–Wives, mothers, or homemakers. No other definition available.

LIBERAL–Focus-group-tested adjective that must precede any idea or person that you don't like.

LOVE OFFERING–Money sent to God by way of True Christian™ television that buys watches and jewelry for the minister that the person sending the money could never afford.

MATERIALISM–Something wicked done by people other than True Christians™. (*See* Jews.) Massive personal wealth among leaders of organizations you support, however, is simply evidence of God's Favor.

MEDIA–No such thing. Always "biased, liberal media." Responsible for teenage pregnancy, illiteracy, sexual addictions, earthquakes, and the breakdown of the family.

MILITANT–Ideas contrary to your own. Examples of inappropriate use: militant pro-lifers, militant antigays, and militant Christians.

NONPARTISAN–An impartial group that always votes Republican. (*See* Christian Coalition.)

PERSECUTION–What occurs when someone dares to question your position. Examples of "persecution" include investigative journalistic reporting, any lawsuit filed against a True Christian™ organization by the ACLU, any communication from someone you have said is going to Hell, have harassed by fax or phone, or have "misrepresented" in your fund-raising materials. This is something that can only be done *to* you, not *by* you.

PHYSICIAN–Any doctor, except those who perform abortions. Physicians who perform abortions are "abortionists," "baby killers" or "targets."

RADICAL–Applied to anyone who disagrees with you. Thus, "radical" homosexuals, "radical" feminists, "radical" environmentalists. True Christians™ are not radical, they are "committed," "called," and "focused."

REPUBLICAN–*See* God.

SINNERS–People who don't belong to your church.

SO-CALLED–Used to preface beliefs or rights purportedly important to other people.

SOCIAL ENGINEERING (syn. "social experimentation," when used to allow sodomites to run wild in the military)–Term for the "activist agendas" of political opponents. Opposite is the "natural God-given plan" as defined only by True Christians™.

SPECIAL RIGHTS–Focus-group-tested term referring to any right enjoyed by True Christians™ that gay and lesbian Americans are after.

SUPREME COURT APPOINTMENTS–Varying definitions. "Clearing the court of judicial activists," if president is Republican. "Stacking the court with a liberal agenda" if president is Demon-crat. In either case, picking who will appoint our president.

10 PERCENT–A lie about the percentage of the population that is gay or lesbian popularized by Militant Radical Homosexual Activists, when in fact True Christian™ organizations have "proven" the figure is closer to 1 percent. Send a $1,000 Love Offering to Pat Robertson for an explanation as to how 1 percent of the population is responsible for the destruction of the family and civilization.

THOUGHT CRIME–An attempt to outlaw your beloved right to hurl invective and hatred in the Lord's name. Any hatred expressed against you, however, is Persecution and should, of course, be illegal.

TOLERANCE–The first step in turning your children into sodomites.

WILL OF THE PEOPLE–Used only when the public votes your way. Acceptable method of denying constitutional rights of minorities. Never used when public opinion is against you (i.e., abortion, doctor-assisted suicide, etc.).

glossary